# Digital Multimodal Composing

SECOND LANGUAGE ACQUISITION

*Series Editors*: **Professor David Singleton**, *University of Pannonia, Hungary* and Fellow Emeritus, *Trinity College, Dublin, Ireland* and **Professor Simone E. Pfenninger**, *University of Zurich, Switzerland*

This series brings together titles dealing with a variety of aspects of language acquisition and processing in situations where a language or languages other than the native language is involved. Second language is thus interpreted in its broadest possible sense. The volumes included in the series all offer in their different ways, on the one hand, exposition and discussion of empirical findings and, on the other, some degree of theoretical reflection. In this latter connection, no particular theoretical stance is privileged in the series; nor is any relevant perspective – sociolinguistic, psycholinguistic, neurolinguistic, etc. – deemed out of place. The intended readership of the series includes final-year undergraduates working on second language acquisition projects, postgraduate students involved in second language acquisition research, and researchers, teachers and policymakers in general whose interests include a second language acquisition component.

All books in this series are externally peer-reviewed.

Full details of all the books in this series and of all our other publications can be found on http://www.multilingual-matters.com, or by writing to Multilingual Matters, St Nicholas House, 31-34 High Street, Bristol, BS1 2AW, UK.

SECOND LANGUAGE ACQUISITION: 167

# Digital Multimodal Composing

Connecting Theory, Research and Practice in Second Language Acquisition

**Matt Kessler**

MULTILINGUAL MATTERS
Bristol • Jackson

DOI https://doi.org/10.21832/KESSLE6673
Library of Congress Cataloging in Publication Data
A catalog record for this book is available from the Library of Congress.
Library of Congress Control Number: 2023048800

British Library Cataloguing in Publication Data
A catalogue entry for this book is available from the British Library.

ISBN-13: 978-1-80041-667-3 (hbk)
ISBN-13: 978-1-80041-042-8 (pbk)

**Multilingual Matters**
UK: St Nicholas House, 31-34 High Street, Bristol, BS1 2AW, UK.
USA: Ingram, Jackson, TN, USA.

Website: https://www.multilingual-matters.com
Twitter: Multi_Ling_Mat
Facebook: https://www.facebook.com/multilingualmatters
Blog: https://www.channelviewpublications.wordpress.com

Copyright © 2024 Matt Kessler.

All rights reserved. No part of this work may be reproduced in any form or by any means without permission in writing from the publisher.

The policy of Multilingual Matters/Channel View Publications is to use papers that are natural, renewable and recyclable products, made from wood grown in sustainable forests. In the manufacturing process of our books, and to further support our policy, preference is given to printers that have FSC and PEFC Chain of Custody certification. The FSC and/or PEFC logos will appear on those books where full certification has been granted to the printer concerned.

Typeset by Deanta Global Publishing Services, Chennai, India.

# Contents

|  | Acknowledgements | vii |
|---|---|---|
|  | **Part 1: Introduction and Theoretical Support** | |
| 1 | Introduction | 3 |
| 2 | Key Theories and Concepts | 12 |
|  | **Part 2: Research on DMC and Language Learning** | |
| 3 | Writing Processes | 29 |
| 4 | Outcomes and Evidence of Learning | 45 |
| 5 | Teachers' and Students' Perceptions | 61 |
| 6 | Individual Differences | 77 |
|  | **Part 3: Pedagogical Applications** | |
| 7 | DMC Tasks and Activities | 95 |
| 8 | Assessment | 109 |
| 9 | Conclusion and Future Research Directions | 121 |
|  | References | 133 |
|  | Index | 148 |

# Acknowledgements

This book could not have come to fruition without the efforts of many. First and foremost, I am grateful to Multilingual Matters for giving me this opportunity and platform. Similarly, I am thankful to my editor, Laura Jordan, as well as the anonymous reviewer. Both provided me with careful assistance and important feedback on earlier drafts. I am also very grateful to my friend and collaborator, Jungmin Lim. It is her work on multimodal composing that first piqued my interest in the subject matter years ago. A special thank you also goes to my doctoral research assistant at the University of South Florida, Benjamin Puterbaugh, who graciously assisted me in conducting some of the background research for this book.

Last but certainly not least, thank you to Mim, who continues to support me and my career. Without her, this book would not be possible.

# Acknowledgements

# Part 1
# Introduction and Theoretical Support

# 1 Introduction

**Introduction to Multimodality and Digital Multimodal Composing (DMC)**

*Multimodality* is a concept that refers to people's use of two or more *modes* for the purpose of communicating an intended message or meaning. *Modes* are the potential resources that a person leverages for conveying that meaning. Notably, numerous modes are available for communicative purposes, and common modes include those that are *linguistic* in nature (e.g. written text, speech), *visual* (e.g. images, colors), *aural* (e.g. music, soundtracks), *gestural* (e.g. actions, hand gestures, facial gestures) and *spatial* (e.g. the layout or arrangement of items) (Jewitt, 2006; Kress, 2003, 2010). Therefore, when a person combines two or more of these modes and uses them in a purposeful manner, their communications can be described as multimodal. Examples of multimodal communication (or multimodality) can be found all around us, as they are an integral part of the fabric of daily life. Common examples in society include advertisements, comics and graphic novels, flags, magazines, newspapers, posters and street/traffic signage.

To illustrate how different modes are often used or combined into a multimodal genre for specific communicative purposes, let us take street/traffic signage as an example. In the United States, for instance, there are a number of different types of street/traffic signs, and these signs often consist of particular combinations of modes. Modes used in traffic signage might include a combination of colors (e.g. red, yellow or orange), shapes (e.g. an octagon, triangle, rectangle or square) and linguistic text (e.g. *stop, yield, road work ahead, right lane closed ahead*). Although many traffic signs may include linguistic text, in some cases, they may not. For example, some signs might consist of a color, shape and an image in place of linguistic text (e.g. an orange, diamond-shaped sign, with an image of a man digging or working). In all such instances, those who designed these signs carefully selected these combinations of modes, and they were united into a single multimodal genre with the intention being to communicate a specific message to a particular audience. In the case of street/traffic signage, the purpose of combining these different modes is to communicate messages to motorists so that they are aware of what to do in a given situation (e.g. to stop, to yield to oncoming traffic and to slow down due to the presence of construction workers).

It is important to note here that, although examples of multimodality can be found almost everywhere, the use and meanings of modes are often socially shaped by the different cultures or communities who use them (Kress, 2010). For instance, in continuing with the example of street/traffic signage, different countries often use different systems of linguistic text on their signs based on the specific language(s) used in those countries. This, of course, might seem rather obvious. However, some readers might be surprised to learn that depending on the country, traffic signs might also be shaped differently and/or use different colors to convey their messages. In Japan, for instance, stop signs may be red in color; yet, instead of being octagon shaped (as in the United States and many other countries), they may be in the shape of an inverted triangle (see Figure 1.1). Relatedly, in countries such as Australia, Cambodia and the United States, highway and wayfinding signs are often green in color with white text. Meanwhile, in other countries such as China and Spain, they may be blue in color with white text.

Of course, this phenomenon of modes having varied meanings based on the cultural context applies to other genres beyond street/traffic signage as well. For example, with flags, the same color, symbol or shape may signify relatively different meanings depending on the country and the people who designed the flag. Relatedly, even an individual mode itself, such as color, can convey vastly different messages depending on the culture and people who are interpreting it. For instance, in most countries, wearing a green-colored hat often carries no specific meaning. However, to many people in China, wearing a green hat signifies that one's spouse or partner has been unfaithful to them. Thus, clearly,

**Figure 1.1** Stop signs in the United States and in Japan (Images from Openverse.org. English 'stop sign' by Clover Autrey CC-BY 2.0. ©; and Japanese 'Kanji Traffic Signs – Kyoto, Japan' by Gary CC-BY 2.0. ©

understanding the significance of both individual modes and combinations of modes (i.e. multimodality) is an important aspect of daily life. This is because multimodal awareness and literacy may have a number of implications that range from the more severe (e.g. a potential traffic accident) to the less serve, yet, admittedly, somewhat embarrassing in nature (e.g. wearing a green hat while traveling in China).

Interestingly, although multimodality has existed in practice for hundreds of years among human societies, only more recently has the concept gained momentum as a topic of scholarly inquiry. In particular, academic interests in multimodality can be traced directly to the work of the linguist M.A.K. Halliday and the publication of his 1978 book titled, *Language as a Social Semiotic*. In his book, Halliday explored the use and learning of languages in different social and cultural contexts. One of the central ideas of Halliday's text is that language is fundamentally social in nature, and also, that humans make or produce meaning in a myriad of creative ways. As Sun *et al.* (2021) have noted, this idea was subsequently taken up by a number of scholars who are interested in what is now called *social semiotics*, a field that investigates how people co-construct meaning by leveraging various modes for different communicative purposes (e.g. Hodge & Kress, 1988; Jewitt, 2003, 2006; Kress & van Leeuwen, 1996, 2001). Consequently, Halliday's (1978) work became highly influential and sparked a scholarly movement on the topic of multimodality, which greatly impacted a number of academic fields, including communication, education and applied linguistics.

When it comes to applied linguistics in particular, the subfield of second language acquisition (SLA) has seen an increase in research interest involving multimodality in recent years (e.g. Block, 2013; Guichon & McLornan, 2008; Kessler, 2022a; Perez, 2020; Yi & Angay-Crowder, 2016). Of course, this makes sense because as a field, SLA researchers are typically interested in investigating issues pertaining to the learning of second and/or additional languages, including how people acquire and communicate with those languages. Interestingly, despite the publication of Halliday's *Language as a Social Semiotic* in the late 1970s, the topic of multimodality itself received almost no attention within the domain of SLA until a publication by Christine Tardy, which appeared in 2005. In her study, Tardy (2005) explored multimodality by examining how four, multilingual writers manipulated different modes when designing slideshow presentations via PowerPoint in an effort to convey various meanings and to express their disciplinary identities. Importantly, in her work, Tardy (2005: 335) also remarked on the increasingly digital and multimodal nature of academic writing, and she rightly predicted that 'visual modes will continue to grow in importance for multilingual writing research'. Tardy's piece is now considered a seminal publication in the area of SLA scholarship, and it is credited with spurring many SLA researchers' interest in the topic (see Lim and Kessler [2023] for a research timeline on multimodal writing and SLA, which spans from 2005 to 2022).

When it comes to SLA research involving multimodality, perhaps no group of scholars has been more active than those who research issues related to second language (L2) writing. This, in part, is due to the fact that Tardy herself is a prominent L2 writing scholar, whose 2005 study was published in an academic journal that is devoted to researching first language (L1) and L2 writing (i.e. *Computers and Composition*). Additionally, Tardy's original statement about academic writing tasks becoming increasingly digital and multimodal was also noted by others, who made relatively similar observations around the same time period (e.g. Molle & Prior, 2008; Nelson, 2006). In the years that followed, such works spurred an interest not only in exploring multimodal writing, but also in investigating the related topic of *digital multimodal composing*, which is the subject and focus of the current book.

*Digital multimodal composing* is a term that refers to the design or production of a digital genre, in which an individual integrates linguistic text with one or more non-linguistic modes (Kessler & Marino, 2023). Studies such as Lim and Polio (2020) have demonstrated that in today's world, DMC is a common practice across both academic and professional settings, with numerous digital genres being widely used for different communicative purposes. Such digital genres include (but are not limited to) blogs, websites, digital posters and brochures, slideshow presentations (e.g. PowerPoint), e-portfolios and video projects. Because of DMC's ubiquitous nature, in recent years, the topic of DMC has received growing attention, and it has subsequently developed into a relatively robust area of inquiry. This attention has come from scholars in a number of fields. Primarily though, those who have investigated DMC have tended to work in fields such as computer-assisted language learning (CALL), educational technology or L2 writing (e.g. Dahlström, 2022; Guichon & McLornan, 2008; Hafner, 2015; Jiang, 2017; Li, 2022; O'Byrne & Murrell, 2014; Zhang *et al.*, 2023).

Due to DMC's growing relevance and the important roles that digital genres and digital literacy now play in both academic and professional success, the current book is devoted to exploring the topic of DMC and, specifically, exploring DMC's use and effects in the areas of L2 teaching and learning. The next section further expands on the intended aims of the book, including its primary audience and the various topics that will be covered.

## Aims, Audience and Chapter Previews

This book examines the topic of DMC by focusing on the intersections of theory, research and practice in the domain of SLA. Specifically, the current book is intended for graduate students, faculty, practicing teachers and researchers who work with L2 learners in a range of diverse instructional contexts. Apart from those who work in the field of SLA, this book is also intended to serve as a resource for those who currently work or have backgrounds in fields such as applied linguistics, CALL, educational technology or L2 writing. However, in this book, particular attention is given to the researching and teaching of L2 writing, since most DMC scholarship to date has tended to be conducted in this area.

Regarding multimodal writing or DMC, a number of scholars have been skeptical of the idea of integrating multimodality into the L2 classroom. Some researchers have even suggested that focusing on non-linguistic modes in one's teaching may detract from or stifle language development (e.g. Manchón, 2017; Qu, 2017). However, there is now strong evidence – which will be discussed throughout this book – to refute such claims. For example, there is historical evidence that humans' use of different modes may naturally evolve over time. For one, scholars in other disciplines such as law have documented how people have moved from relying primarily on oral language to written language as the basis for everyday legal practices (see Coulthard *et al.*, 2017). Second, apart from the historical evidence of such modal changes, there is also ample research which now demonstrates that multimodal writing and DMC tasks and activities have the capacity to positively influence different aspects of the SLA process. Finally, there is also the current state of human communications to consider, which, as discussed, are increasingly digital and multimodal in nature. To put it bluntly: L2 teachers and researchers can no longer simply ignore such realities.

As such, this book presents a theoretically and methodologically diverse introduction to key theories and scholarship supporting DMC's use, along with practical pedagogical tips and tools for adopting DMC in the L2 classroom. The book consists of nine chapters, which are divided into three major parts. These three parts correspond to the title of the book, which involve considerations of theory (Part 1), research (Part 2) and practice (Part 3). These three parts are further described in the following paragraphs.

Part 1 of the book is titled 'Introduction and Theoretical Support', and it consists of two chapters: this chapter (Chapter 1) the 'Introduction' and Chapter 2 which covers the topic of 'Key Theories and Concepts'. Chapter 2 introduces readers to the influential theories and concepts that previous researchers have adopted when investigating issues pertaining to DMC. The chapter begins with a discussion of why theory is vital for engaging in both research and pedagogical activities, particularly when it comes to facilitating grounded and informed decision-making practices. Seven theories are discussed in total: systemic functional linguistics, social semiotics, multiliteracies, interactionist approaches, sociocultural theory, activity theory and metacognition theory. In addition to explaining these seven key theories that have featured prominently in DMC research, also discussed are a handful of influential concepts that have guided aspects of scholarly activity, including the concepts of *design*, *remix* and *collective scaffolding*.

Part 2 of the book is titled 'Research on DMC and Language Learning', and it consists of four content chapters (Chapters 3–6). These four chapters each cover different popular topics that have been investigated by researchers – published through the end of 2022 when this book was written – in which researchers have collected data from participants in a classroom or lab setting, rather than secondary research (e.g. synthesis articles). Notably, a majority of the research presented in Chapters 3–6 is qualitative in nature; however, there are also numerous studies discussed in these chapters that adopt quantitative or mixed methods.

The chapters in Part 2 follow a consistent internal organizational structure. Chapters 3–6 each consist of four subparts. The first subpart includes an introduction, which defines the topic area for the readers, along with introducing readers to important terms and forecasting the major themes that will be discussed in the chapter. After the introduction, the second section in each chapter is titled 'Research: Key Findings'. In this section, prominent studies are presented and reviewed in connection with the chapter's topic. Each study is described in considerable detail, including highlighting features of the authors' research aims, methods, learner populations involved in the study and the findings. The next section in each chapter is titled 'Implications for Researchers', which provides a discussion of important points to consider if/when conducting research on the topic in the future. These implications are drawn directly from the studies previously reviewed within the chapter, often with comments pertaining to the studies' designs. Finally, each chapter in Part 2 closes with a section titled 'Implications for Teachers'. As the title implies, this section draws on the studies that were presented in the chapter as a means of discussing the more practical and pedagogical-related concerns related to the chapter's topic.

In terms of the content of these research-oriented chapters in Part 2, the first chapter is Chapter 3, which addresses the topic of learners' 'Writing Processes'. This chapter explains the process movement in L2 writing scholarship, in which many researchers have (partly) shifted their attention away from examining students' final written products, and instead, moved toward analyzing the process of writing itself, seeing it as a fruitful site for student expression, discovery and growth. Specifically, Chapter 3 concentrates on a handful of studies in which researchers have attempted to tap into different aspects of L2 learners' writing processes as they engage with various DMC tasks and activities.

Following the discussion of L2 learners' writing processes, Chapter 4 examines the important topic of 'Outcomes and Evidence of Learning'. As mentioned, some scholars have been concerned about multimodality's potentially negative side effects on (linguistic) L2 learning outcomes.

However, there are now a number of studies that have the capacity to speak to DMC's effectiveness in promoting facets of SLA. Chapter 4 examines a collection of such studies, and primarily, it examines those articles that have explored DMC's influence on the development of oral and/or written linguistic modes.

Chapter 5 addresses 'Teachers' and Students' Perceptions' of DMC. In the fields of applied linguistics, education and SLA in particular, research that examines aspects of teachers' and learners' beliefs has long been a staple of academic work. This is because understanding different stakeholders' perceptions has been seen as instrumental both in terms of encouraging buy-in and also in terms of understanding any potential differences that may exist between the two groups' vantage points. Therefore, Chapter 5 examines studies that have explored teachers' and students' perceptions of DMC tasks when they are implemented in a range of diverse instructional settings.

In the final research-focused chapter of Part 2, Chapter 6 turns to a discussion of DMC's influence on 'Individual Differences'. Individual differences (IDs), which refer to 'learner traits and characteristics that may have an impact on learning processes, behaviors, and outcomes' (Li et al., 2022b: 3), are a rapidly growing area of interest within the field of SLA. This is because numerous IDs have been demonstrated to impact the process of language learning. Chapter 6 focuses on a select few IDs that have been examined within the realm of DMC scholarship. In particular, this chapter discusses research that has investigated DMC's impact on L2 learners' identity, motivation and metacognition.

The final part of the book, Part 3, is titled 'Pedagogical Applications', and it consists of three chapters (i.e. Chapters 7–9). In this part of the book, the more practical, teaching-related applications of the research that was reviewed in Chapters 3–6 are discussed. The first chapter in Part 3 is Chapter 7 titled 'DMC Tasks and Activities'. This chapter provides readers with a systematic review of popular DMC tasks and activities, including those covered in the current book and in the published literature more broadly. This review serves as a means of providing readers with a more thorough understanding of current pedagogical practices with DMC. After providing an overview of commonly used tasks, the chapter moves on to describe several DMC tasks and activities in more detail, including giving suggestions for how instructors might implement them in various contexts with different learner populations. The chapter closes with a list of digital resources for teachers to further explore if/when implementing DMC tasks.

Chapter 8 is titled 'Assessment' and, as the name suggests, is devoted to covering the challenging issue of assessing students' DMC projects in the L2 classroom. To facilitate the nexus between theory, research and practice, the chapter begins by providing readers with a brief overview of some of the key literature that has explored issues involving DMC assessment. Next, pedagogical tips and recommendations are provided for adopting either a *product-based* approach or a *process-based* approach for assessing learners' DMC creations. In this chapter, the design and creation of rubrics are also discussed for readers to consider. Similar to Chapter 7, Chapter 8 concludes with a list of digital platforms, tools and other resources that teachers might consider when engaging in DMC assessment in the future.

The final chapter of the book, Chapter 9, is titled 'Conclusion and Future Research Directions'. Based on the prior content chapters in the book (i.e. Chapters 2–8), this final chapter is devoted to discussing some of the major research and pedagogical needs that have been identified, with a specific eye toward connecting theory, research and practice. In particular, several future research directions (called 'research tasks') are proposed. These research tasks are meant to serve as a starting point for graduate students, faculty and L2 teachers who may be interested in conducting DMC-oriented research in a range of contexts.

## Conclusion

Before concluding this introductory chapter, it is worth noting here that throughout this book, the terms *task* and *activity* are referred to synonymously as one and the same (as some readers may have noticed already). This is primarily due to the fact that definitions of the term 'task' abound in both the applied linguistics and SLA literature. In particular, researchers who have advocated for a task-based language teaching (TBLT) approach have defined or operationalized the term 'task' as being a very specific type of activity that must meet multiple criteria, such as being meaning focused and having an authentic context (see Ellis, 2017; Ellis & Shintani, 2014). However, for a book such as this one, the use of 'task' in accordance with TBLT literature is somewhat problematic. This is because what may be authentic and meaningful in one instructional context may not be in another (e.g. a digital video project may be more or less meaningful in the different contexts in which this book is currently being read). Therefore, throughout this book, the term 'task' will not be used in keeping with TBLT approaches, and instead, 'task' and 'activity' will be used interchangeably. If teachers and instructors are interested in TBLT approaches, I encourage them to consider whether those tasks/activities described in this book can truly be defined as meaningful and authentic both within and beyond the walls of their classrooms.

In closing, the current book is intended to serve as a useful guide for those who are interested in the nexus of DMC and SLA, including graduate students, faculty, teachers and researchers who work with L2 learners in a myriad of contexts. Importantly, I note here that, without question, a number of studies have been omitted from this book. However, this book is intended to showcase some of the most prominent empirical studies and scholarly work on the topic of DMC within the scope of SLA. Additionally, I have carefully selected studies that I feel have the capacity to help facilitate connections between theory, research and practice. Thus, this book is not intended to serve as an exhaustive account of any/all research on the topic of DMC to date.

In the end, as mentioned, it is my hope that this text will serve as a starting point for those who are interested in gaining a foundational level of understanding of the key areas involved in DMC scholarship. However, as will be discussed throughout this book, despite the fact that DMC is presently a lively area of research activity, there is still much to be done. Thus, I close this introductory chapter by encouraging readers to further investigate and interrogate those theories, research methods and pedagogies discussed throughout this book.

# 2 Key Theories and Concepts

**Introduction**

When it comes to understanding digital multimodal composing (DMC) in the context of second language acquisition (SLA), both research and pedagogy in this topic area have spanned multiple academic disciplines, often being interdisciplinary in nature. For instance, scholars who are interested in understanding the potential affordances and drawbacks of DMC's use for second language (L2) teaching and learning purposes have often drawn on the work of researchers who work in fields such as applied linguistics, communication, education and psychology, along with various subdisciplines which sit at the intersection of these fields, such as educational technology, computer-assisted language learning (CALL) and L2 writing. In the domain of SLA in particular, it is important to note that researchers have typically invoked a handful of key theories and concepts for the purpose of investigating DMC's use, and for making sense of its subsequent influence on various aspects of L2 learning processes and outcomes.

For many individuals who are reading this text, such as (under)graduate students, language teachers or early-career researchers, one vital question that they might pose is *Why does theory matter?* As a growing body of literature suggests, many teachers and students often feel this way, in particular that there is a major disconnect between theory and practice. Some might even question the value of theory and research altogether for a number of (understandable) reasons, which often involve the more practical side of seeing how theory and research apply to one's own classroom practices (see Sato & Loewen, 2019; Sato et al., 2022). However, in many of the social sciences, including applied linguistics and SLA, theory is a vital consideration for both research and pedagogically oriented activities.

In terms of research, theories – which are statements about natural phenomena that have the capacity to explain as well as predict such phenomena (VanPatten & Williams, 2015) – are a vital means of grounding and motivating one's work. Thus, based on people's prior observations of how L2 learning happens in a given situation or context (e.g. in the classroom), people then develop certain theories and sets of predictions. If, in fact, these theories and predictions are true, then they should manifest again in similar situations in the future. For researchers who adopt *quantitative* methods in their research designs (i.e. using larger sample sizes and statistics in an effort to generalize the results of their studies), their experiments often take a theory as a starting point and as a means of testing certain hypotheses. Conversely, for researchers who approach their work using *qualitative* methods (i.e. using only one or a handful of participants, with more explicit focus and attention paid to the experiences and actions of individuals), theory is also an integral part of the research process. This is because in qualitative research, theory is the guiding lens through which complex social interactions and L2 learning may be understood – for more on the similarities and differences between quantitative and qualitative research methods, see Gao *et al.* (2022) and Paltridge and Phakiti (2015).

Finally, theory is undoubtedly a vital consideration for practicing language teachers. This is because theory, research and practice are intimately intertwined. Theory is typically the driving force behind most research. This research, in turn, often directly influences a number of aspects of educational practices, namely, impacting textbook and materials design (Tomlinson, 2022); the use of different teaching methods or approaches such as communicative language teaching and task-based language teaching (Brown & Lee, 2015); and the use of different pedagogical tasks, activities and exercises in the classroom (Polio & Kessler, 2019). Therefore, by understanding theory, a teacher has a legitimate means of justifying and explicating *why* he or she is taking certain actions inside (or outside) of the language classroom. Additionally, as discussed, theories often originate from observations that are made in practice. This relationship between theory, research and practice is not fixed or hierarchical, but is both dynamic and cyclical in nature. Thus, the work that teachers do in their classrooms is equally as important in this regard.

Due to the critical nature of theories and the powerful role they play in influencing aspects of research and practice, this chapter introduces readers to the key theories that researchers have leveraged when investigating DMC's use in a variety of L2 learning contexts. In this chapter, particular attention is paid to those theories that appear in later chapters of this book involving DMC research (i.e. Chapters 3–6) and when discussing teachers' pedagogical practices (i.e. Chapters 7 and 8). As mentioned, DMC scholarship has often been interdisciplinary in nature. Therefore, this chapter discusses theories that derive from a number of fields such as applied linguistics, communication, education, psychology and SLA. In total, seven theories are discussed: systemic functional linguistics (SFL), social semiotics, multiliteracies, interactionist approaches, sociocultural theory, activity theory and metacognition theory.

In addition to explaining these theories that have featured prominently in DMC-oriented research, a handful of key concepts are also discussed in this chapter. These concepts, which include *design*, *remix* and *collective scaffolding*, are not full-fledged theories in the sense that they attempt to account for or predict naturally occurring phenomena. Instead, these concepts are specific terms that researchers have frequently employed in their studies, either when discussing aspects of implementing DMC tasks and activities in the classroom (i.e. design and remix), or when describing aspects of L2 learners' interactions when they engage in a DMC task with a partner(s) (i.e. collective scaffolding).

Finally, before proceeding to the next section, it is worth noting that because these theories and concepts are described in considerable depth in this chapter, they will not be discussed in detail in later chapters. In subsequent chapters, these key theories and concepts are only briefly mentioned if/when an author's study was motivated by one of them. Thus, for additional details, readers are encouraged to revisit this chapter and/or an author's original work.

## Key Theories

In this section, seven different theories that have been invoked for the purposes of motivating and exploring DMC's use in both research and pedagogy are discussed. As mentioned, these theories are quite diverse, both in terms of the fields that they originated from and in terms of their scope and the different types of phenomena that they attempt to describe.

### Systemic functional linguistics

It is important to begin this section with SFL. This is because the concept of multimodality is generally regarded as emerging from this theory (Jewitt, 2006; Kress, 2003). In his seminal book-length work, the linguist M.A.K. Halliday (1978) explicated his theory of human communication, socialization and interactions. Notably, Halliday's theory of SFL (also see Halliday, 1985) has greatly influenced numerous aspects of research and teaching over the years, including genre-based approaches to teaching L2 reading and writing (see Accurso & Walsh Marr, 2024), and of course, research involving the foci of this book, multimodal writing and DMC.

In his theory of SFL, Halliday (1978) was chiefly concerned with exploring and understanding how humans use different forms of communication to achieve different social and functional purposes. Other popular theories of education and language acquisition/use at the time, such as behaviorism, typically saw language as being learned and used through a cycle of conditioning and reinforcement. In contrast, Halliday posited that human communication was a complex social system in which human beings constructed meaning by making different types of agentive choices. In this sense, in a subsequent publication, Halliday

(1985: xiv) noted that SFL is 'a theory of meaning as choice'. Specifically, Halliday regarded language as a social semiotic system (i.e. a system of signs and symbols), in which humans use and produce language according to three main metafunctions: *ideational*, *interpersonal* and *textual*. As Halliday and Matthiessen (2004) describe, these metafunctions explain the different types of semiotic choices that humans make when expressing ideas (ideational); how humans interact with others by attempting to establish relationships and assume different roles (interpersonal); and how humans leverage specific discourse features and cohesive devices in order to convey their meanings (textual).

Readers of this book should note that Halliday's three metafunctions often surface in some areas of applied linguistics research such as multimodal discourse analysis (see D'Angelo & Marino, 2024). However, in regard to research involving multimodal writing and DMC, SFL is typically referred to in a very broad sense. That is, researchers typically only briefly reference Halliday (1978) and his work with SFL, and then move on to discuss the concept of multimodality, along with other L2 studies that have investigated DMC. However, readers should note that Halliday's theory of SFL is considered important because of his discussions of both modality and his conceptualization of human communication as a set of resources. These ideas from Halliday's work subsequently motivated a sizable amount of research on other types of modes that people use to communicate, including how individuals may combine modes in order to produce various meanings.

## Social semiotics

Building upon Halliday's work with SFL is the theory of social semiotics. In both developing and advocating for social semiotics' use, key figures include Carey Jewitt from the field of education, along with linguists Robert Hodge, Gunther Kress and Theo van Leeuwen (e.g. see publications by Hodge & Kress, 1988; Jewitt & Kress, 2003; Kress, 2010; van Leeuwen, 2005). Similar to SFL, the theory of social semiotics is interested in investigating how humans create meaning. However, social semiotics is more broadly concerned with understanding communication and meaning in all their forms, including all available modes and signs, while SFL tends to place more of an emphasis on the linguistic mode. As Kress (2010) further explains:

> The core unit of semiotics is the *sign*, a fusion of form and meaning. Signs exist in all modes, so that all modes need to be considered for the contribution to the meaning... In a social semiotic account of meaning, individuals, with their social histories, socially shaped, located in social environments, using socially made, culturally available resources, are agentive and generative in sign-*making* and communication. (Kress, 2010: 54, italics in original)

Thus, the foundational principle and idea behind social semiotics is that language is inherently a social phenomenon, rather than merely a biological one. Because of this, the theory is chiefly concerned with understanding how society, social interactions and the contexts of communication influence both sign use and meaning (Jewitt *et al.*, 2016).

As mentioned, social semiotics is interested in understanding and accounting for all meaning-making modes and signs, with the concept of multimodality at the forefront. Therefore, building upon Halliday's (1978) three metafunctions of *ideational, interpersonal* and *textual* meanings, in social semiotics, these meanings have been expanded as a way of understanding (1) how ideas and meanings are represented in multimodal communications; (2) how relationships are formed between a designer (i.e. the producer of the communication) and the receiver; and (3) how multiple modes are orchestrated (Kress & van Leeuwen, 2001). As Sun *et al.* (2021: 5) explain, with social semiotics, the notion of agency and design is critical, as humans use 'signs and codes as semiotic resources', among which, they 'are able to make selections to create meaning in a particular context'.

Similar to SFL, when it comes to research involving DMC, social semiotics is again typically referenced in a very general sense. For example, in many DMC studies, researchers often only briefly acknowledge the theory in their introduction or literature review sections, and they cite it as an influential theoretical paradigm. This is particularly the case for DMC-oriented studies that investigate aspects of L2 learners' writing processes and how students orchestrate or manipulate multiple modes while composing (see Chapter 3).

## Multiliteracies

Along with SFL and social semiotics, perhaps no theory has impacted research involving multimodal writing and DMC more than that of *multiliteracies*. Notably, while some researchers have occasionally referred to multiliteracies as a 'framework', most often, multiliteracies has been conceptualized and understood as a theory of literacy (e.g. Cole & Pullen, 2010; Serafini & Gee, 2017). The term *multiliteracies* was coined by the New London Group in 1996. This group consisted of a collection of 10 scholars, primarily from education-related disciplines, who convened in the early-to-mid 1990s to discuss and consider the future of literacy pedagogy. Members of the New London Group who may be familiar to those in applied linguistics and SLA include Courtney Cazden, Bill Cope, Jim Gee, Mary Kalantzis and Gunther Kress. In their paper, the New London Group (1996) explored the general mission of education, the evolving nature of literacy practices and how to better prepare students to succeed beyond the classroom as members of a modern society.

Importantly, in the New London Group's work, they clearly described the changing nature of human communications, which they saw as growing ever more multimodal in nature. As they stated:

> Increasingly important are modes of meaning other than Linguistic, including Visual Meanings (images, page layouts, screen formats); Audio Meanings (music, sound effects); Gestural Meanings (body language, sensuality); Spatial Meanings (the meanings of environmental spaces, architectural spaces); and Multimodal Meanings... Reading the mass media for its linguistic meanings alone is not enough. (New London Group, 1996: 80)

Due to the changing nature of literacy, the New London Group (1996) advocated for the teaching of what they called *multiliteracies*, or specifically, for teachers to move beyond privileging the linguistic mode alone. As Cope and Kalantzis (2009) note, what this means is that for contemporary teaching to be successful, it requires teachers to adopt a new pedagogy of multiliteracies. Instructors, then, must embrace the concept of multimodality and teach their students how to read and write a variety of multimodal texts, in addition to teaching students how to understand, manipulate and design intended meanings with linguistic *and* non-linguistic modes.

In terms of influencing research, the New London Group's (1996) paper is frequently referenced by those who are interested in multimodal writing and DMC. In fact, in the subsequent research-oriented chapters of this book (i.e. Chapters 3–6), the theory of multiliteracies is referenced far more than any other theory. In total, 36.1% of the studies reviewed in this book discuss multiliteracies as being one of the theoretical drivers behind their work (with the next closest theory being social semiotics, which is referenced by 13.9% of the studies' authors).

## Interactionist approaches

Unlike SFL, social semiotics and multiliteracies – all of which discuss the concept of modality or multimodality explicitly – interactionist approaches do not. In fact, of the theories discussed in this chapter thus far, interactionist approaches is the first to originate from scholars who work primarily in the field of SLA. At the outset, it is important to note that interactionist approaches are not a unified theory. Rather, interactionist approaches are a collection of theories and hypotheses that have come to be closely associated over the years. This collection consists of the interaction hypothesis (e.g. Long, 1981, 1996), the input hypothesis (e.g. Krashen, 1981, 1982), the output hypothesis (e.g. Swain, 1985, 1993, 1995) and the noticing hypothesis (Schmidt, 1990).

To begin, the driving force behind interactionist approaches is the work of applied linguist Michael Long (1981), who drew upon components of Krashen's (1980) input hypothesis. In his work, Long (1981) theorized that in order for language acquisition to occur, comprehensible input was of the utmost importance, with comprehensible input referring to oral speech or written text, which, through interaction, could be modified by interlocutors so as to be understandable for L2 learners. However, following Long's original hypothesis in 1981, applied linguist Merrill Swain (1985, 1993, 1995) contended that receiving comprehensible input was not enough to lead to the acquisition of a target language (TL). This assertion came from Swain's own research and observations involving L2 French learners in Canadian immersion programs. As Swain noted, although these students' receptive abilities in the L2 of French (i.e. their reading and listening skills) developed strongly, their ability to produce the TL was not as fully developed. This led Swain to put forward the output hypothesis, which contends that L2 learners must also be pushed to produce the TL so that they can test hypotheses, receive feedback and then produce modified output, accordingly.

Finally, in addition to the output hypothesis, applied linguist Richard Schmidt (1990) proposed the noticing hypothesis. Schmidt's theory contended that in order for SLA to occur, learners need to consciously notice aspects of the input that they receive. That is, L2 learners must be aware of the linguistic forms, pronunciation, etc., that they are hearing or reading in the TL, and how such forms are either similar to or different from those forms in their first language (L1). Based on these developments and critiques of his 1981 interaction hypothesis, Long (1996) modified his hypothesis to integrate these aspects of output and noticing, with particular emphasis placed on how interaction between individuals encourages input, output and the opportunity for learners to consciously notice aspects of the TL.

In terms of DMC-oriented research, when invoking interactionist approaches or related aspects such as the noticing hypothesis, DMC scholars typically do not reference these hypotheses as a means of supporting DMC's use. Instead, interactionist approaches are usually discussed in studies that explore the use of DMC projects that are conducted collaboratively between pairs or small groups of students. That is, when adopting interactionist approaches as a theoretical framework, researchers are interested in investigating aspects of L2 learners' interactions as they collectively work on an assigned DMC task. This includes examining aspects of the output that L2 learners produce when collaborating, along with examining the extent to which collaborative DMC tasks may promote the conscious noticing of different features of the TL. For more on interactionist approaches, readers are encouraged to see Gass and Mackey (2020).

## Sociocultural theory

The next theory discussed is sociocultural theory, a popular theory of human learning, which stems from the work of psychologist Lev Vygotsky (1978). Sociocultural theory contends that the development of human beings' mental processes is a fundamentally mediated process. Similar to interactionist approaches, sociocultural theory asserts that human development often occurs as a result of human-to-human interaction. However, unlike interactionist approaches, sociocultural theory is a theory of general human learning and development, rather than a theory that is specific to SLA. Additionally, and perhaps more importantly, while interactionist approaches stress the importance of oral- or text-based interactions between two or more interlocutors, sociocultural theory is more multifaceted in its conceptualization of how learning may occur. For instance, as Lantolf *et al.* (2020) note, sociocultural theory also sees human development as possible through individuals' use and leveraging of cultural artifacts and concepts. These artifacts and concepts may be concrete and tangible in nature (e.g. published books, or technologies created by humans such as computers); however, these artifacts and concepts can also be intangible or symbolic in nature (e.g. language itself). That is, although people are able to learn via human-to-human interactions, people can also learn from using and interacting with such culturally constructed artifacts as books and computers. Crucially, sociocultural theory also argues that people can learn from themselves or from within. This may occur by talking inwardly to oneself in what is often called *private speech* (see Wertsch, 1985), thereby leveraging the cultural artifact of language (a conceptual tool) for the development of higher psychological processes.

Sociocultural theory has been highly influential in a number of fields, including applied linguistics, education and SLA. As referenced, sociocultural theory is a complex theory of general human development and, as such, a number of key components have been researched in the area of L2 writing. These include the concept of the *zone of proximal development*, which refers to the area of a learner's current knowledge state, and the ultimate state of learning or knowledge that can be achieved via the assistance of an expert or more knowledgeable person (e.g. Aljaafreh & Lantolf, 1994). Also emerging from Vygotsky's work is the concept of *collective scaffolding*, which is often considered to be an interpretation and extension of Vygotskian sociocultural theory (this concept will be described in further detail in the section titled 'Key Concepts'). In terms of DMC research, when drawing on sociocultural theory, authors typically reference Vygotsky (1978), along with the related concept of collective scaffolding. Similar to those DMC-oriented studies involving interactionist approaches, this is often done in studies where the researchers are examining the use of collaborative DMC tasks, typically as a means of investigating how students interact and learn from each other during a jointly produced DMC activity.

## Activity theory

Springing directly from Vygotsky's (1978) work with sociocultural theory is another prominent theory, activity theory, which has been widely explored in the fields of applied linguistics, education and SLA. In particular, activity theory stems from the psychologist and philosopher Aleksei Leont'ev (1978, 1981), who was a colleague and contemporary of Vygotsky's. The theory was also further developed in later years by Yrjö Engeström (1987, 1999), whose work with activity theory is most often cited in scholarship within the areas of SLA and L2 writing. In Engeström's writings on activity theory, he defines humans' behavior and social activities as a highly complex system with numerous elements that intersect and influence one another. According to Engeström, human beings' activities can be better understood as an *activity system*, which is visualized in Figure 2.1.

As shown in Figure 2.1, Engeström conceptualized human activity as a triangle, in which there is a *subject* (appearing on the left side of the image), with this subject representing a person or agent who performs some sort of action. As Park and De Costa (2015) have illustrated, in the case of L2 writing, the subject can be understood as a writer. This subject (or writer) then attempts to achieve a specific outcome or goal, which is conceptualized as the *object* (e.g. the object might be writing a paper or completing a specific writing assignment given by one's teacher). However, as the subject attempts to pursue this object, their actions are influenced by many other culturally constructed and socially mediating factors. For instance, in the pursuit of the object, the subject might leverage various types of *artifacts*, which can be conceptual (e.g. language, concepts) or physical in nature (e.g. different technologies or tools such

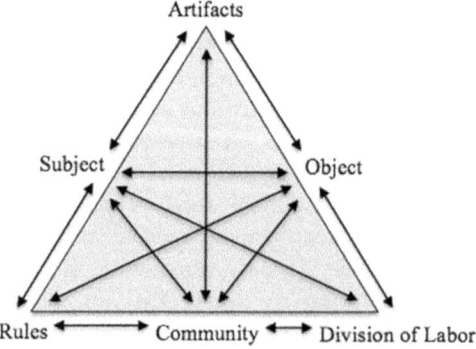

**Figure 2.1** Activity system (adapted from Engeström, 1999)

as a laptop, the internet or books). Within the activity system as well, different *rules*, a *community* and perhaps a *division of labor* occur. For example, there may be specific *rules* that influence the subject's actions. In the case of writing, rules are likely to include the teacher's grading criteria and field-specific genre conventions, all of which the subject must follow when completing the writing assignment. In addition to these rules, the subject will also likely be influenced by the *community* he or she is a part of, such as one's classmates, peers and friends. Lastly, a *division of labor* may also occurs if the writer seeks support (e.g. guidance from a tutor) or if the workload is divided up in some manner (e.g. engaging in collaborative writing with one or more persons).

Thus, as a theory, activity theory is focused on understanding how an individual's actions, behaviors and learning may be influenced by a host of phenomena. Within L2 writing and DMC studies more specifically, researchers have adopted activity theory as a means of understanding how L2 writers are influenced not only by social factors, but also by cultural artifacts. With DMC and technology-oriented studies especially, primary attention has been paid to activity theory's category of artifacts, as researchers have attempted to understand how different artifacts such as technologies and digital tools may shape aspects of individuals' writing behaviors.

## Metacognition theory

The final key theory discussed in this section is metacognition theory, which was originally developed by educational psychologist John Flavell (1979). Broadly speaking, Flavell described metacognition as people's conscious awareness of their own thinking. Informally, metacognition is often described by many as *thinking about thinking*. Since the time when Flavell proposed the theory, numerous other scholars have researched metacognition, and it has subsequently developed into a multifaceted theory (and corresponding model) that can be leveraged for comprehending the nature of human cognition, including understanding how human beings exert influence over and control their own awareness when engaging in different tasks (e.g. Brown, 1978; Pintrich, 2002, 2004; Schraw & Dennison, 1994). Today, most researchers agree that the construct of metacognition consists of two major components: *metacognitive knowledge* and *metacognitive regulation* (see the model depicted in Figure 2.2).

The first component of metacognition theory is the construct *metacognitive knowledge*, which is shown on the left side of the model in Figure 2.2. This construct refers to people's general awareness of their own consciousness and thoughts (Pintrich, 2002). However, as the figure shows, a person's metacognitive knowledge is thought to consist of multiple dimensions or suborders, including *declarative knowledge, procedural knowledge* and *conditional knowledge*. These three dimensions

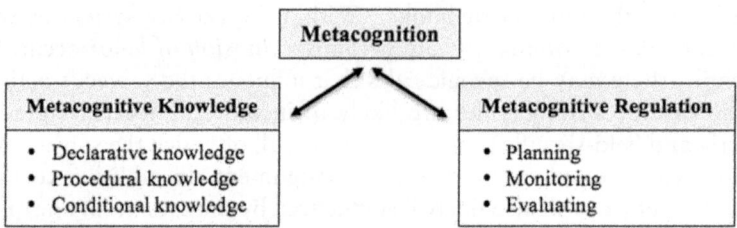

**Figure 2.2** A model of metacognition theory (designed by the author; developed from works such as Brown [1978], Flavell [1979], Negretti and McGrath [2018], Pintrich [2002] and Schraw and Dennison [1994])

refer to 'what we know (declarative knowledge), how to apply it (procedural) and why it is relevant to the current learning conditions (conditional)' (Negretti & McGrath, 2018: 15). Thus, these three dimensions are associated with what people report being aware of, that is, people's capacity to discuss their awareness of 'about', of 'how' and of 'why' (Schraw & Dennison, 1994: 114). To help illustrate these three dimensions, let us consider the act of writing a paper. For example, writers with strong metacognitive knowledge of a target genre might be able to verbalize their declarative knowledge of the genre's audience, or about the rhetorical and linguistic features that are typically characteristic of the target genre. With procedural knowledge, writers might be able to verbalize how they would approach organizing content and structuring information within the target genre. Regarding the third suborder, conditional knowledge, writers might also be able to explain how/why they would perform certain actions. For instance, this might include explaining how/why changes in various elements might impact their composing processes (e.g. how different audiences might influence aspects of their writing such as language use or the inclusion of content).

As shown on the right side of the model in Figure 2.2, the second component of metacognition theory is the construct of *metacognitive regulation*. As Schraw and Dennison (1994) explain, metacognitive regulation refers to the aspect of control, including how people direct their awareness or assert control over different sub-processes while performing a task. This includes *planning, monitoring* and *evaluating* task outcomes. Returning to the previous example of composing a target genre, when regulating their metacognition, writers may reflect on their awareness of the genre prior to performing the writing task (i.e. planning). Additionally, writers may consciously keep in mind specific features of the genre while they are writing (i.e. monitoring), and they may also consciously review their work and overall performance once they are finished with the writing task (i.e. evaluating).

As the preceding examples suggest, metacognition theory is a complex theory of human consciousness. In the domain of L2 writing in particular, the theory has shown great potential, helping researchers understand different aspects of L2 writers' awareness of different writing tasks, along with how learners mobilize (or do not mobilize) their awareness before, during and after a writing task. As regards research involving DMC, too, a handful of researchers have adopted metacognition theory as a means of exploring learners' general metacognition when performing DMC tasks, the types of skills that learners bring to such tasks and more. Lastly, metacognition theory has also been leveraged as a means of interrogating how using linguistic and non-linguistic modes may help promote conscious attention to features of different genres (see Chapter 6 for example studies).

## Key Concepts

As discussed in the opening section of this chapter, apart from several prominent theories that have been invoked for the purposes of investigating different aspects of DMC's influence in the L2 writing classroom, there are also a number of key concepts associated with DMC research and pedagogy. These key concepts or terms are not like the aforementioned theories, which attempt to explain and even sometimes predict certain social and psychological phenomena. Instead, these key concepts are frequently used to describe different aspects of DMC's implementation, ranging from aspects involving students' composing processes to the way in which learners work together during different DMC activities.

### Design

The first key concept that is addressed in this section is *design*. As discussed in the New London Group's (1996) highly influential work on multiliteracies, traditionally, the concept of literacy has been understood as learning to read, write and interpret print-based linguistic texts. However, due to the proliferation of digital technologies and digitally based media, in today's world, becoming a literate individual now involves much more than simply being able to master linguistic forms. In addition to linguistic forms, this includes being able to read, comprehend and manipulate visual modes (e.g. images), aural modes (e.g. music), gestural modes (e.g. gestures) and spatial modes (e.g. layouts). Thus, multiliteracy itself requires individuals to be able to leverage and orchestrate multiple modes simultaneously, or in other words, to be able to *design* intended meanings.

In the New London Group's (1996) work, they refer to the concept of design in two different ways. First, they discuss the concept in terms of how it relates to teachers, or how instructors approach and design their curricula and activities. However, the second way in which they discuss design has been picked up and adopted much more broadly in scholarship involving multimodality and DMC. Their second use of the term *design* refers to human beings as communicators, with design being used to describe 'semiotic activity as a creative application and combination of conventions (resources)' (New London Group, 1996: 74). As Kress (2010: 28, italics in original) goes on to explain: '*Design* is the process whereby the meanings of a designer (a teacher, a public speaker... participants in everyday interactions) become *messages*. *Designs* are based on (rhetorical) analyses, on aims and purposes of a rhetor...'. In other words, because human beings have individual agency, they proactively choose from a number of socially available modes when producing a message. The messages that people produce are (often) carefully constructed or designed, but these designs are also likely to be influenced by various factors such as genre conventions.

In the context of L2 writing research, researchers who are interested in DMC frequently mention the concept of design when referring to the writing processes that L2 learners engage in when working on a DMC task and activity. Often, DMC researchers will use the term *design* synonymously with other words such as *compose* or *composing*. That is, learners can be seen as designing and/or composing a specific message during a DMC task such as a digital poster, in which they draw on a number of socially available modes to produce intended meanings.

## Remix

The next key concept discussed is that of *remix*. Many L2 writing teachers may already be familiar with this term, albeit in a different sense. Traditionally, remix has been considered a type of pedagogic activity that is used in many L2 (and L1) writing classrooms, in which a teacher asks students to take an existing assignment that they have created (typically for the same class). Students are then asked to transform and change that assignment into a new form or genre. For example, in an English for Academic Purposes course, students might be asked to take an existing research paper that they have written. Then, students might be asked to remix their research paper into a poster that is intended for a generalist (i.e. non-specialist) audience. Similarly, students might be asked to take their lengthy master's thesis or doctoral dissertation, and to turn it into a *3-minute thesis*, which is a video-based presentation with one static slide (see Hyland & Zou, 2021).

However, in multimodal writing and DMC, the term *remix* itself has been used in a related but different manner. (Admittedly, this repurposing [or remixing] of an existing, established term is somewhat confusing.) Yet, when pertaining to digital technologies, Knobel and Lankshear (2008: 22) have defined remix as a 'means to take cultural artifacts and combine and manipulate them into new kinds of creative blends'. As Hafner (2015: 487) further explains, remix with DMC can be understood as 'the creative appropriation and repurposing of existing digital texts', which serve as 'an expressive resource in… multimodal compositions'. In a digitally based modern society and culture, remix is seen as a common practice (e.g. with individuals remixing music and movie/film trailers). Thus, as regards DMC, remixing is seen as a particular type of process or action, in which designers (or writers/composers) take existing cultural artifacts that have been produced by others. People then edit and combine these existing artifacts in creative ways in order to produce new products and meanings.

Specifically, when it comes to research that investigates topics involving DMC, readers should note that remix is most often used in this sense – that is, as a type of process or action that involves the borrowing and repurposing of others' work – as opposed to the more traditional definition of remix, which involves turning one's own original work into a new genre. Therefore, in DMC scholarship, researchers often discuss the concept of remix, particularly in studies that are interested in investigating aspects of L2 learners' writing processes and products. Such researchers are interested in understanding how learners blend, layer and repurpose others' existing works (e.g. music, videos) to create something new such as a film or documentary.

## Collective scaffolding

The third and final key concept discussed in this section is *collective scaffolding*. As noted earlier, the concept of scaffolding itself, which refers to providing carefully attuned assistance and support to a learner, has often been interpreted as stemming from Vygotksy's (1978) work on sociocultural theory. This is primarily because of Vygotsky's discussion of the zone of proximal development, along with how he conceptualized the nature and space in which learning occurs. It is important to note here that some scholars actually disagree about the extent to which sociocultural theory equates scaffolding with the zone of proximal development (see Xi and Lantolf [2021] for a discussion). Nevertheless, numerous researchers have drawn on Vygotsky's work as a means of theoretically motivating and expanding this concept of scaffolding into what is known as *collective scaffolding*.

The concept of collective scaffolding comes from the work of Donato (1994), in which the researcher conducted a small-scale qualitative study that investigated students of L2 French at an American university. In his work, Donato cited Vygotsky (1978: 42) as one of the primary theoretical drivers behind his research. At the time, Donato noted that most research involving the topic of scaffolding tended to focus on how teachers supported their students, yet no studies had looked at how L2 learners supported each other when collaboratively engaging in different activities. Therefore, Donato set out to observe three L2 French students as they worked together in class on a variety of small-group tasks. Through observing the students' interactions, Donato noted that his focal learners took turns taking on different roles during oral tasks, supporting each other and also providing positive and negative evidence for what was possible (or not possible) in the L2 French. Thus, Donato (1994: 51) concluded that students engaged in 'collective scaffolding', as they were clearly 'capable of providing guided support to their peers during collaborative L2 interactions'.

In terms of this book and DMC research, collective scaffolding is frequently mentioned by researchers in studies where the focal participants are engaging in some type of pair or group work. In fact, collective scaffolding is often seen as one of the primary benefits of having learners engage in collaborative writing tasks. Specifically with DMC, these peer-to-peer discussions also have the capability of providing a window into how learners process and make sense of multiple modal resources, along with how L2 learners collaborate and learn from each other when engaging in a DMC task.

## Conclusion

As discussed throughout this chapter, there are a myriad of key theories and concepts that scholars have used to motivate their research on DMC, and to understand various facets of DMC's influence on L2 learning processes and outcomes. With theory, in particular, although some of these theories (e.g. metacognition theory) are not specific to the field of SLA, their very scope and nature make it possible for them to inform our understanding of a number of phenomena. Also in regard to theory, it is important to note here that most researchers typically do adopt solid theoretical rationales as a means of underpinning their research activities. However, there are also a number of published studies that appear to lack theoretical grounding, sometimes only referring to multimodality rather generally or vaguely (i.e. by referring to previous studies in the area of multimodal composing rather than mentioning specific theories or theoretical constructs). As discussed in the opening section of this chapter, theory is a vital means of supporting both research and pedagogic activities for a number of reasons. Therefore, for those who wish to conduct research in the area of DMC in the future, they are strongly encouraged to ground their work in a specific theory. This issue is revisited in Chapter 9, which serves as a conclusion and also discusses future directions involving aspects of theory, research and practice. In the interim, readers are encouraged to take note of the different theories and concepts adopted by researchers in the chapters that follow.

# Part 2
# Research on DMC and Language Learning

# 3 Writing Processes

**Introduction**

In the field of second language (L2) writing, the investigation of learners' *writing processes* has been an area of considerable scholarly activity over the past few decades. As Matsuda (2003) and others have noted, early first language (L1) composition and L2 writing studies traditionally placed much of the focus squarely on learners' written products. That is, researchers were primarily interested in investigating aspects of the written texts that students produced, such as students' use of rhetoric, various linguistic features and the accuracy of grammatical forms. However, in the 1980s, the field of L1 composition was swept by a new process movement, which penetrated both research and pedagogy circles (see Applebee, 1986; Tobin, 1994). This process movement shifted the focus away from learners' products and more on their writing processes, viewing the act and process of writing itself as a fruitful site for personal expression, discovery and growth. This movement, in turn, greatly influenced L2 writing research and teaching in the 1990s, and since that time, it has continued to be an important topic of inquiry.

In terms of L2 writing, researchers have been interested in investigating a broad range of phenomena related to learners' writing processes. Such phenomena include but are not limited to exploring learners' various social and (meta)cognitive strategies when engaging in different writing tasks and genres (e.g. Kessler, 2020a, 2021b, 2021c; Sato, 2022; Wenden, 1991); understanding how students adopt and integrate different source-based materials with research-oriented tasks (e.g. McCulloch, 2013; Neumann *et al.*, 2019); and examining how the manipulation of different task conditions (e.g. planning time; individual versus collaborative writing) impacts aspects of learners' writing processes (e.g. Michel *et al.*, 2022; Ong, 2014; Storch, 2019).

On the heels of the process movement, there was also an increase in scholarly activity focusing on the theoretical affordances of the writing process. Notably, researchers such as Williams (2012) have remarked that unlike speaking, the act of writing is typically slower paced in nature, and the enduring record of words on a page (or computer screen) has the capacity to promote numerous aspects of second language acquisition (SLA). For instance, the act of engaging in writing may promote an explicit or conscious noticing of different target language forms (see Schmidt, 1990), and it may help learners recognize gaps in their awareness or interlanguage. Importantly, most early-stage or lower-proficiency learners often engage in *learning-to-write* activities, in which they are taught how to spell and how to utilize and manipulate different grammatical forms in highly controlled situations. However, as students progress and develop in their L2 proficiency, they often transition to *writing-to-learn* activities. In these activities, the writing process is used as a means for students to learn new ideas and engage in critical thinking (see Leow, 2020). Finally, when completed either independently or collaboratively, researchers have demonstrated that the writing process can be a rich site for L2 learning (see Leow & Suh, 2022; Li & Zhang, 2023; Storch, 2022).

As highlighted, much has been learned about L2 learners' writing processes, particularly when engaging with traditional monomodal texts. However, in response to this research, Stapleton and Radia (2010) argued that despite such progress, L2 writing researchers and practitioners needed to devote more attention to investigating the impact of technology on the writing process. Subsequently, this argument was viewed as especially relevant for research involving digital multimodal composing (DMC) because little was understood as to how students manipulated and orchestrated different modal resources in order to produce various meanings when engaging with multimodal genres. Consequently, over the decade that followed, this call was answered, particularly by computer-assisted language learning (CALL) researchers and L2 writing scholars who were interested in DMC.

This chapter focuses on the topic of DMC and L2 learners' writing processes. Specifically, the chapter concentrates on a small number of studies in which the researchers have attempted to tap into different aspects of language learners' writing processes as they engage with various types of DMC-based tasks and activities. When reviewing studies for this chapter, only empirical studies with an overt focus on DMC were included. That is, some research has tangentially addressed issues related to technology, multimodality and students' writing processes. For example, a number of early collaborative writing studies explored aspects of students' writing processes with web-based platforms and tools such as wikis (e.g. Kessler & Bikowski, 2010; Kessler *et al.*, 2012). Although such studies often required participants to engage with multiple modes, the studies' authors typically provided little (if any) overt discussion of students' use of multiple modes apart from linguistic text or oral discussions, respectively. Therefore, such studies have been omitted from the review that follows.

When analyzing the body of literature that has investigated L2 learners' DMC processes to date, this scholarship has tended to fall into two major categories or themes: (1) *exploratory analyses of learners' general DMC processes* and (2) *studies investigating transformation and/or remix practices*. Each of these themes is further described in the next section. When discussing each theme, four or five studies are presented in considerable depth in order to highlight features of the studies, including their instructional contexts, DMC tasks, research methods and findings. Notably, these studies were selected because they speak to different facets of each theme. All studies are presented chronologically by date of publication (i.e. from oldest to newest).

## Research: Key Findings

### Exploratory analyses of learners' general DMC processes

The first theme pertains to studies that focus on analyzing learners' DMC processes in general. Typically, such studies have tended to be framed as more exploratory in nature, with the goal of the research being to broadly investigate how L2 learners use or leverage different modes during the composing process. Of the two themes presented in this chapter, most DMC process research tends to fall into this area.

The first study in this category is by Yang (2012). In her research, Yang adopted a case study design to explore two L2 English learners' multimodal composing processes as they engaged in a digital storytelling project. The learners were English majors in an undergraduate course in Taiwan, who were enrolled in a teacher education program. Grounded in social semiotics (e.g. Kress, 2003, 2010), the researcher was specifically interested in understanding how English language learners approached the design of their digital stories, and how they constructed their texts to deliver intended messages. Yang (2012: 224) noted that both of her focal learners had 'abundant experiences using technologies' prior to the course. For the course's final project, students in the class were asked to produce a digital story that illustrated their participation as members of an online community. Students were first shown examples of digital stories and multimodal webpages, and they were then given options to use for completing their projects, such as Cyberlink Power Director, iMovie and Microsoft Moviemaker. On finishing their projects, students were required to present their stories to their classmates and also to orally narrate their multimodal composing processes.

To understand students' composing processes, Yang (2012) analyzed students' final digital storytelling projects, their oral narrations and other supporting documents (e.g. students' planning notes and storyboards). She also conducted follow-up interviews with the participants. When coding the data, Yang (2012: 225) focused on 'participants' selection and orchestration of multimodal resources' in their stories. In her findings,

Yang reported that the two focal participants integrated various multimodal resources into their stories, such as voice narration, linguistic text, still images, background music and animation. Importantly, when employing these resources, the students did not randomly adopt or arrange them, but rather, they strategically orchestrated different modes based on their intent to produce desired effects (e.g. evoking emotions from their audience). The two writers were also clearly able to articulate their intentions as to why they used modes for different purposes. In her conclusion, Yang noted the purposeful nature of students' mode use, and she also highlighted the pedagogical utility of the assignment, which promoted critical self-reflection.

Similar to Yang (2012), Nishioka (2016) also investigated students' composing processes and engagement with a digital storytelling task. At the time of her study, Nishioka noted that when it came to prior DMC research, digital storytelling had traditionally been investigated as an individual learning activity. Therefore, motivated by sociocultural theory (Vygotsky, 1978), her study set out to investigate the collaborative dialogue that occurred when students worked together on a DMC task. Set in the context of a two-year college in South Korea, Nishioka recruited three students who were majoring in L2 Japanese to participate in the study. The L2 proficiencies of the learners varied and included a beginner, an upper beginner and an upper intermediate-level student. Together, the three focal students completed an assignment for a course called 'Tourism Japanese' (Nishioka, 2016: 42). The assignment required them to demonstrate both their Japanese language proficiency and their content knowledge by crafting a digital story to describe a popular tourist destination. The project involved multiple stages, including learners' developing their topic (e.g. brainstorming with mind maps), researching content, taking/collecting pictures, outlining their story and using storyboards, and developing and editing their composition. Unfortunately, the author did not specify the specific software and digital tools used for completing the project.

To analyze learners' collaborative dialogue, Nishioka (2016) operationalized the construct by looking at language-related episodes (LREs), or instances in which the students engaged in explicit oral discussions of grammar, vocabulary or spelling issues (see Swain & Lapkin, 1998). The researcher collected multiple sources of data, including observations, audio-recordings of students' interactions, stimulated recalls and students' final DMC composition. In her findings, Nishioka (2016) reported that the three students produced a total of 135 LREs, which mostly pertained to vocabulary (60%) or grammar (20%). Nishioka provided examples of how different modes (e.g. linguistic text, images) elicited discussion among the students, prompting them to scaffold each other by providing assistance when needed. Nishioka also designed an individualized post-test to analyze the students' retention rates of 98 items they discussed while collaborating. Interestingly, their retention rates mirrored their proficiency levels, with the beginner retaining 0% of the items, the upper beginner retaining 29.6% and the upper intermediate-level student retaining 71.9%. Importantly, Nishioka's study demonstrates the utility of having learners collaboratively engage in DMC tasks, and how different modes may generate discussion. It also points to the relative utility (and potential drawbacks) of having L2 learners with such varied proficiencies complete tasks together, since the lowest proficiency student appeared to retain nothing from his interactions.

Smith *et al.* (2017) is the next focal study, which sought to explore aspects of adolescent L2 learners' DMC processes. The study took place in an eighth-grade English classroom in the Southern United States with three participants. As part of the English course, the students completed a four-week project called 'My Hero' (Smith *et al.*, 2017: 10), which required them to read a short memoir before constructing a multimodal presentation in which they selected a person from their own life whom they considered a hero. The multimodal presentation required the students to interview their hero, and then create a presentation in which they had to include information about their hero's background, synthesize their interview, discuss how it connected to the memoir they had read and include any final personal reflections. The students were instructed to use Microsoft PowerPoint to complete the assignment. Because the focal students had different L1 backgrounds, the researchers conducted the interviews using their L1s and heritage languages. Therefore, the researchers were specifically interested in understanding students' translingual practices and multimodal *codemeshing*, which they defined as 'how bilingual students strategically draw on multiple languages, images, music, voice recordings, animations, and other design features to make meaning' (Smith *et al.*, 2017: 9).

Adopting a case study design, the researchers collected data such as screen-recordings of students' composing processes, observations, interviews in which they asked students about their designs, along with students' final multimodal projects. For data analysis, the authors first openly coded the data, time-stamping students' actions and processes (for video data). They also obtained inter-coder reliability for 25% of their coding (91.8%), something that is relatively uncommon among qualitative studies of this nature. Finally, they engaged in member checking, a process by which they conferred with their participants to confirm/deny their conclusions. Smith *et al.*'s (2017) findings illustrate that all students engaged in codemeshing, strategically using their heritage languages and other modes (e.g. images, sound). However, their comparisons of the three participants' cases showed varied processes for different students. For instance, one participant's processes were primarily text driven, while another's was visual driven. The authors illustrated this by graphically representing the total number of minutes each student spent on the project engaging with different modes (e.g. engaging in an image search, image design, text design, voice recording). The findings highlight the unique nature of how different learners approach the DMC writing process. The authors also noted that the DMC project allowed students to develop both their heritage languages and the target language simultaneously.

Moving from a K-12 to a university context, Yeh and Tseng (2020) investigated 52 L2 English learners' DMC processes as they engaged with augmented reality (AR) technology (i.e. technology that blends virtual elements with real-world contexts). In the study, intermediate-level English as a foreign language (EFL) learners were enrolled in a course at a Taiwanese university that was called 'Multimedia English' (Yeh & Tseng, 2020: 29). The course required students to produce content using an AR application (app). The app was self-developed by the researchers; however, they also commented on the utility of other AR apps such as ARKit, CoSpace and Makar. Using the AR app, students were required to create content that would enable tourists in Taiwan to use their phones to find specific sites of interest and to interact with those locations once they arrived. None of the participants had experience with AR apps before the study. The project was lengthy in duration, spanning 18 weeks and consisted of numerous phases. For instance, students needed to select a tourist location and conduct background research (Week 3). They also had to create virtual elements for the tourist spot (Weeks 4–17) and include textual information, photos, audio and video. In Week 18, students published their apps, and they also completed a post-study survey and wrote reflection essays about their experiences participating in the project.

The data collected during the project was then analyzed using content analysis in four stages: coding, categorizing, describing and interpreting the results. Yeh and Tseng (2020) provided inter-coder reliability for their coding (0.89), but it is unclear whether this reliability figure accounts for part or all of their dataset. In the findings, Yeh and Tseng focused on describing how their EFL learners adopted different modes, in addition to how learners used modes for different functional purposes. Students' rationales for using different modes were supported by examples extracted from their reflection essays. For instance, many students often adopted a variety of visual modes (e.g. images, animations) to direct viewers' attention to specific points of interest. Students also used audio (e.g. background music) to arouse different emotions. Similar to the study by Yang (2012) described earlier, Yeh and Tseng's (2020) work showcases students' purposeful employment of different semiotic resources to convey specific meanings and engage their audience. Although AR apps have infrequently been used in DMC research, the researchers close by noting their potential affordances, especially getting students to learn about and establish connections with an audience.

The final study described in this subsection is Kessler (2020a). Unlike the previous studies in this chapter which address the direct application of teacher-assigned DMC projects in the classroom, this study explored students' DMC processes and composing strategies beyond the classroom. A case study design was used to explore two L2 English learners from China, who were in the first semester of their graduate programs in the United States. The study's goal was specifically to understand student-initiated technology use, including how students used different technologies, tools and modes when completing their writing assignments. As such, after the two focal participants had been given their first writing assignments by their course instructors (e.g. a research proposal), various data were collected to explore the students' composing processes, including their course syllabi, process logs (in which students discussed their pre-writing strategies), screen-recordings of the learners' actual composing practices and follow-up stimulated recalls and interviews.

To account for the complexities of students' writing processes, activity theory (Engeström, 1987, 1999) was adopted. Data were coded using a two-cycle coding approach in relation to activity theory (i.e. looking for themes within the theory's main tenets of mediating *artifacts*, *rules*, *community*, etc.). In the findings, both participants adopted different technologies and tools, which were an indispensable part of their writing processes. Notably, this study highlights students' idiosyncratic use of different modes. For instance, one participant used various combinations of colors and fonts (e.g. red font, red underlining, yellow highlighting) to signal different meanings in the digital articles and documents she read. These multimodal combinations then facilitated her writing processes by enabling her to quickly locate different types of information and to integrate that information into her writing assignment. Thus, this study is noteworthy in that it highlights student-initiated uses of semiotic resources for different purposes.

### Studies investigating transformation and/or remix practices

Apart from those studies that have explored L2 learners' DMC processes more generally, the second theme consists of studies that have examined learners' transformation or remix practices. As discussed in Chapter 2 which covered the topic of *key theories and concepts*, the concept of *remix* has (rather confusingly) been used differently by some L2 teachers and researchers. Traditionally, the concept of remix has been understood as a type of pedagogic activity that is used in many L2 (and L1) writing classrooms, in which a teacher asks students to take an existing assignment they have created (typically for the same class) and to transform that assignment into a new genre (e.g. taking an argumentative essay and turning it into a poster). However, when it comes to DMC, the term *remix* has been used by researchers to reference a particular type of process or action, in which writers/composers take existing cultural artifacts that have been produced by others. Students then combine and edit others' artifacts in creative ways to produce new products. To avoid confusion in this section, the term *transformation* is used to refer to the former meaning (i.e. the processes of students taking an assignment that they produced and turning it into a new genre). Conversely, the term *remix* is used to refer to when writers sample and rework existing cultural materials produced by others.

Digital media, especially online, affords learners numerous meaning-making resources from which to draw, including songs, sounds, images and videos (see Lessig, 2008). In turn, writers can use digital tools to gather and remix these existing works (e.g. creating a short movie by gathering still images, moving video clips and a soundtrack). Thus, both studies of transformation and remix share a common thread, in that scholars have primarily been interested in understanding how students' take something old and turn it into something new.

Hafner (2015) was one of the first SLA-oriented studies to explore this topic. In his study, he examined the remix practices of EFL learners who were enrolled in an undergraduate English for science course in Hong Kong. For the course, students were required to complete a digital video project in groups, in which they had to choose a scientific topic, conduct background research, collect and analyze data, and then report their findings to a non-specialist audience. The genre of their videos was supposed to reflect a scientific documentary. The specific tools used for creating the videos were not discussed; however, students were required to post their videos on YouTube once completed. The researcher, who also taught the science course, adopted a case study design and collected data over a 15-month span. In addition to collecting students' digital videos, he conducted focus groups with 18 students to learn more about their remix practices and communicative strategies.

Although Hafner (2015) collected numerous videos, he selected just two to showcase in his study. These videos were analyzed using the multimedia data analysis tool MAXQDA. During the analysis, Hafner broke down and coded the videos based on different shots, examining what modes were used and where they originated from (e.g. an existing movie, song). In his findings, Hafner reported on his students' remix practices, which most frequently consisted of appropriating stock images and footage. The students, as in Yang (2012) and Yeh and Tseng (2020), were purposeful in their employment of different modes. For instance, some students stated that using existing footage simply 'enhance[d] the visual quality of the video' (Hafner, 2015: 496). Other students felt that stock images and video enhanced the authoritativeness or strength of their voices (i.e. making their videos appear more legitimate). Interestingly, some students also remixed different modes to create hybrid genres. For example, one group mixed together the theme music from the film

*Mission Impossible* with their documentary. However, this practice was once again purposeful in nature, as the students were attempting 'to attract the attention of their audience' (Hafner, 2015: 500) in a humorous manner. Based on his findings, Hafner noted that remix can be used strategically in the L2 classroom to generate peer discussion and new kinds of meaning. However, he also noted some of the drawbacks of digital video projects, such as the extended time commitment that was required for students to complete it, along with potential copyright issues that may arise if students post their videos publicly online.

The next study in this category is Shin and Cimasko (2008), in which the researchers investigated students' processes of transforming argumentative essays into DMCs. Motivated by social semiotics, this study took place in an English as a second language (ESL) first-year composition class with 14 students. For the course, students had to create a personal website using the platform Dreamweaver, which would serve as a repository for hosting all of the projects they created during the academic semester. For one of the students' writing assignments, they were given an argumentative writing task, in which they needed to select a topic, take a position and then conduct research to support that position. However, when completing their project, students were specifically asked to transform it into a multimodal composition by integrating non-linguistic modes. Before doing so, the teacher discussed how students might use audio, hyperlinks, images and videos when creating multimodal texts.

In addition to analyzing students' webpages, Shin and Cimasko (2008) collected data in the form of teacher conference notes, in which the classroom teacher met with students to discuss their progress on their compositions. When analyzing students' webpages, the researchers drew on a model proposed by the New London Group (1996). This model was proposed to help researchers understand the different design elements in students' compositions, making suggestions for considering elements such as colors, music and vocabulary. After analyzing the data, the authors reported that most of the students prioritized the linguistic mode over all others. Additionally, some students were hesitant to integrate non-linguistic modes because of what they felt were 'norms of traditional academic discourse' (Shin & Cimasko, 2008: 387). When students did integrate other modes, they tended to be still images, yet these images often mirrored the linguistic content within their texts rather than creating new meanings. Only 1 of the 14 students leveraged audio. In closing, Shin and Cimasko noted the tensions that existed between monomodal and multimodal writing tasks. In particular, they noted that even when explicitly directed to use other modes, their students were strongly influenced by the traditional nature of the argumentative academic essay genre.

In a similar study published nearly a decade later, Cimasko and Shin (2017) conducted a case study of one ESL writer, who transformed an argumentative essay into a multimodal digital video. The study took place in a first-year ESL composition course in the United States. During the semester, students were required to transform an argumentative essay they had written (which the authors referred to as a 'remediation project' [Cimasko & Shin, 2017: 394]), by presenting their arguments in a new manner using digital tools. Students were given the option of using different digital tools and software, including iMovie, Microsoft Moviemaker, Nawmal, PowerPoint and Prezi. The researchers specifically chose to focus on one L1 Russian participant in their findings, since the student 'provided detailed explanations about her choices of modes and designing processes' (Cimasko & Shin, 2017: 396). To investigate the modal choices made by their participant, the researchers collected multiple data points, including the participant's argumentative essay, her final video, observations, field notes and interviews. They conducted interviews on three different occasions, including before, during and after the project.

In analyzing the data, Cimasko and Shin (2017) focused on the different modes the student employed in her video, including any transformational changes that were made when moving from the monomodal to multimodal assignment. To increase the validity of their findings, they triangulated their data, and they engaged in member checking with their participant. Interestingly, unlike their previous study (i.e. Shin & Cimasko, 2008), the authors found that their participant readily adopted different modes when transforming her written essay into a digital video. For instance, the participant identified a link between the argumentative writing genre and a formal oral debate. Therefore, she transformed part of her text into a video that depicted an animated oral conversation between two friends (which also included hand gestures and colors). Cimasko and Shin (2017) also detailed some of the linguistic changes that occurred during the transformation. For example, the student's video script contained more sentences than her original argumentative essay. However, the sentences in her video tended to be far shorter in terms of average number of words used. The video also contained less nominalization and a larger number of contractions. Cimasko and Shin closed their study by noting how the transformation assignment forced their participant to think about the complex relationships between genre, audience and language use, and specifically, how context shapes one's rhetorical decisions.

The final study outlined in this section is Shin *et al.* (2020). The researchers investigated a sixth-grade ESL student's writing processes in an elementary school in the United States. The focal participant in their case study was an L1 Ukrainian speaker. As part of the course, all students were required to create two multimodal projects: to compose an expository essay that explained the scientific concept of the greenhouse effect and to compose an argumentative essay that discussed the banning of guns/weapons. Both texts were to be constructed using multiple modes, with the expository essay created using Microsoft

PowerPoint, and the argumentative text created using the multimedia platform Glogster. Thus, one of the researchers' main goals was to investigate how their focal participant transformed monomodal assignments into multimodal ones, along with how the student attempted to establish intermodal relationships between linguistic text and images. Before engaging in the tasks, the classroom teacher adopted a systemic functional linguistics (SFL) informed-approach to teach the students about the target genres and multimedia authoring tools. The instruction followed an SFL teaching–learning cycle that included deconstructing sample texts as a class, jointly constructing texts through collaborative writing and, finally, independently constructing the projects on their own (see Accurso and Marr [2024] and Rose and Martin [2012] for more).

To analyze the student's writing processes and transformations, Shin *et al.* (2020) collected observations, interviews and the student's DMCs. Once again motivated by SFL, their analyses focused on examining the intermodal relationships that were established between language and images. In their findings, Shin *et al.* stated that their focal participant often adopted (and favored) linguistic, print-based norms despite being encouraged to use other modes for his projects. However, the participant frequently used visuals and images in both his PowerPoint and Glogster compositions, and he primarily used images to create *ideational* meanings, or to describe concrete actions and behavioral processes (e.g. smiling, looking at something). The student also showed a developing awareness of various modes and their potential to create different meanings. Shin *et al.* concluded their study by noting that future research needs to investigate L2 writers' transformation processes using a variety of genres. Pedagogically, they suggested that teachers need to help develop students' metalanguage for talking about different meaning-making resources.

## Implications for Researchers

Based on the previous review of the literature, this section now turns to a discussion of the implications of this research. Specifically, this section discusses important takeaways for researchers, including notes about the previous studies' methods and the need for future scholarship.

Beginning with the methods of DMC writing process research, readers of this chapter likely have noticed that nearly all of the aforementioned studies have tended to be qualitative case studies. As multiple researchers have noted, a case study design has often been favored when investigating L2 learners' writing processes because it affords researchers an in-depth and detailed understanding of one person or a small group of people (see Duff [2008] for more). For writing processes, in particular, a case study allows researchers to gain an understanding of the complexities of L2 learners' decision-making practices, including their intentions, actions and interpretations of their own work. Based on a review of those studies in this chapter, this is clearly evident, as the researchers provided highly detailed descriptions of students' uses of different modes when engaging with DMC tasks.

Research is now needed that adopts quantitative or mixed methods to examine learners' writing processes. Perhaps the closest study in this chapter is Yeh and Tseng (2020), who investigated 52 L2 English learners' DMC processes as they engaged with AR technology. However, while their study did adopt the use of inferential statistics (i.e. paired samples $t$-tests), these tests were used for a different research question that examined learning outcomes rather than aspects of students' writing processes. The SLA research community now has a relatively robust understanding of individualized learner writing processes with DMC. However, little is known about typical or commonly recurring writing processes. For instance, quantitative and mixed methods studies are needed that investigate aspects of learners' writing processes or strategies when engaging in a specific task or activity. Unanswered questions include: What types of modes do learners typically adopt (and/or favor) when engaging in a digital storytelling task (or another DMC task)? What rationales do learners provide for using these modes (and for not using other modes)? Additionally, how do students' use of different modes vary or change depending on the task itself? For example, are there differences in the total number and types of meaning-making resources that learners employ in digital storytelling and slideshow presentations? Likewise, what factors may account for or predict students' mode use in different tasks (e.g. gender, L1, technology experience)? These are only a few sample questions, among many, which might be investigated via the use of quantitative or mixed methods.

In continuing with this focus on prior studies' methods, another note is that even with qualitative case study designs, the duration of such studies has (generally) been very short. Case studies investigating L2 learners' DMC processes have tended to collect data around a single DMC project, which often lasts only a few weeks. Thus, for those who may be more qualitatively oriented in their approaches, studies are needed that adopt longitudinal designs, including methodologies such as ethnography. Of the studies reviewed in this chapter, only Shin *et al.* (2020: 12) reported collecting 'longitudinal ethnographic data'. However, some of the details are a little unclear, such as the number of observations they conducted and the distribution of those observations over the study period. Therefore, future researchers might adopt ethnography as a means of investigating the longitudinal changes that occur in students' DMC writing processes over time. Classroom-based ethnographies could be conducted, in which researchers engage in observations, take field notes and conduct interviews with students and their teachers. Since researchers have reported that some students might be hesitant to employ different non-linguistic modes, especially when transforming monomodal assignments into DMC projects, researchers could attempt to see if these practices remain consistent over time and, if not, what social and/or cognitive factors affect such changes in students' writing processes (for more on classroom-based ethnography, see De Costa *et al.* [2022], Kessler and Maloney [2019] and Maloney and Kessler [2019]).

In moving from broader methodological approaches to the types of data collected, future studies are also needed that collect concurrent or *online* data. That is, many of the studies reviewed in this chapter have typically tapped into students' writing processes by collecting data *after* students have already completed their DMC projects. This has been accomplished through having students complete retrospective questionnaires, write reflection papers or engage in interviews with one of the researchers. Notably, sometimes a tension can exist between self-report data involving what students say (or think) they do versus what they may actually do in practice. Therefore, more studies are needed that adopt screen-capture or screen-recording technologies in combination with other data. For instance, both Smith *et al.* (2017) and Kessler (2020a) collected screen-recordings of students' real-time composing processes. These recordings then served as the basis for a follow-up interview or stimulated recall, in which students were asked about specific actions in their videos and to narrate/describe those actions. In addition to screen-recordings and stimulated recall, researchers may also consider adopting think-aloud protocols as a means of tapping into aspects of students' writing processes. In such instances, students could be asked to orally narrate what they are thinking while composing. For more on think-aloud protocols and related issues, see Bowles (2019) and Leow and Morgan-Short (2004).

In terms of data analyses and outcome measures, it is also worth noting that very few studies have focused on issues pertaining to writing processes in conjunction with different linguistic measures. As discussed throughout this chapter, most studies that have investigated learners' DMC processes have focused on how students leverage different semiotic resources and their rationales for using those modes. Yet, very few studies have accounted for more fine-grained linguistic practices (oral or text based) and changes that occur when students engage in multimodal writing, or when students transform a monomodal composition into a DMC. Both Nishioka (2016) and Cimasko and Shin (2017) are rarities in this regard. In her study, Nishioka investigated the oral LREs that occurred during students' collaborative writing processes. In Cimasko and Shin, the authors analyzed the linguistic features of students' compositions and the changes that occurred when they turned an argumentative essay into a digital video (e.g. by looking at the average number of words per sentence, nominalization and contractions).

Many researchers interested in multimodality have often privileged or fronted non-linguistic modes in their analyses and findings sections, and for good reason. After all, non-linguistic modes such as still images, videos and animations – when combined with linguistic text – are not fully understood in terms of their meaning-making potentials. However, because DMC and multimodal writing are situated within the L2 writing and applied linguistics research domain more broadly, scholarship is also needed that looks at different linguistic measures. Similar to Nishioka (2016), researchers might consider investigating aspects of learners' oral interactions as they engage in collaborative dialogues during the writing process. Future research might investigate the similarities/differences that occur when students work collaboratively on monomodal versus multimodal writing tasks. Do we see the same number, types and resolution of LREs in both monomodal and multimodal tasks? Additionally, do certain DMC tasks/activities prompt increased LRE production (e.g. storyboards versus slideshow presentations)? Relatedly, studies are also needed that adopt text-based measures to investigate DMC. Research is needed that explores L2 learners' transformation processes, specifically how students convert monomodal genres into multimodal ones. When doing so, researchers might consider investigating students' transformation processes using complexity, accuracy and fluency measures (for more, see Polio & Yoon, 2024).

## Implications for Teachers

Most of this chapter has dealt with research-related findings and issues pertaining to the methods and designs of studies. This final section now shifts the focus to classroom-oriented issues, along with the implications of the previous studies when it comes to adopting DMC and teaching L2 writing. This section highlights four implications of DMC writing process research on pedagogical practices.

First and foremost, multiple studies highlighted throughout this chapter have pointed to the notion that DMC tasks may have a positive influence on developing students' awareness of different audiences (e.g. Yeh & Tseng, 2020). This may be even more pronounced when students are required to engage in transformation projects in which they turn a monomodal genre into a DMC project, as suggested by Cimasko and Shin's (2017) study. Thus, writing teachers who are working with upper-intermediate or advanced L2 learners may wish to consider adopting a transformation assignment in their classroom. Since argumentative and expository writing are typically taught in many instructional contexts, these essay types could be the target of a transformation project (e.g. subsequently resulting in a DMC blog post, digital video or wiki page). Such an activity could serve as the basis for discussions about audience, and also how different language forms might need to be used or adjusted based on the intended audience and new digital genre. This type of transformation project may force students to use different types of rhetoric in order to appeal to different audiences, thereby better comprehending the complex relationships between genre, audience and rhetoric.

The second pedagogical implication pertains to students' hesitancy to adopt different modes. This was a recurring issue that appeared in a small number of DMC process studies, in which, despite being given explicit instructions, some students were hesitant to use non-linguistic modes such as animations, images, videos and sound clips. When asked why they were hesitant to use them, students noted that they felt pressure to use linguistic text only because of what they felt were the 'norms of traditional academic discourse' (Shin & Cimasko, 2008: 387). Thus, if a teacher intends to adopt a DMC task, it may be important to anticipate that this could be an issue for some students at the outset. Teachers might try holding pre-task discussions or brainstorming activities with their students about the prevalence of other modes throughout academia in order to help them understand the increasingly multimodal nature of academic and professional tasks (also see Lim & Polio, 2020). For instance, teachers could have students bring copies of their syllabi from other courses, and then circle which assignments require them to use non-linguistic modes. Engaging in this type of activity may help build learners' awareness of the important roles that other modes play in their academic success.

Relatedly, Shin *et al.*'s (2020) study suggests that teachers may need to help develop students' metalanguage for talking about different meaning-making resources. That is, students need to be taught how to strategically think about mode integration and its purpose or role in the overall composition. Teachers may wish to show their students a sample DMC project or target genre, and then break down the different modes with their students. When doing so, teachers can prompt their students to think about various questions, including both *why* and *how* the modes are being used. For example, when integrating a still image, questions might be posed such as: Does including this image advance an argument? Does it evoke an emotion? Does it help promote readers' comprehension by illustrating a complex process or concept? Teaching students the prevalence of non-linguistic modes and giving them tools for thinking about their implementation may help combat the issue of students' hesitancy.

The third pedagogical implication also pertains to setting up the DMC activity, and specifically, whether it should be completed independently or collaboratively. A number of studies have shown that even when engaging in DMC independently, there are a number of affordances (a topic raised in Chapter 4). Nevertheless, Nishioka's (2016) study highlights some of the benefits of having students collaboratively engage in the DMC process. In her study, the focal group of three learners produced a large number of LREs in which they discussed various aspects of the target language, including grammar, vocabulary and style. However, Nishioka's study also illustrates that if teachers want to maximize students' experiences during the writing process, then they must carefully consider how they form student groups. The findings of her study are supported by numerous other collaborative writing studies, which typically suggest that either dyads or groups of three may be the most productive. Perhaps more importantly, L2 learners' proficiencies must also be considered. If teachers have classrooms with highly varied or mixed proficiencies, it will likely be more conducive to have learners of similar proficiencies grouped together (e.g. Storch & Aldosari, 2013). Otherwise, the lowest proficiency learner in the group may become passive and take away relatively little from his or her collaborative interactions (also see Kessler [2019, 2023a] for a related discussion).

The fourth and final pedagogical implication relates to the post-DMC process. After completing their DMCs, many teachers like to have their students post their compositions to a school- or university-based course management system (e.g. Blackboard, Canvas or Moodle). This way, projects can be viewed by other students in the class, and receive comments and feedback. Other teachers, meanwhile, like to have students post their creations to a public venue (e.g. a blog, YouTube), especially if they do not have access to a course management system in their instructional context. However, if posting DMCs in public spaces, both teachers and students need to be extremely careful. As noted in Hafner's (2015) study, if students are engaging in a DMC remix assignment, potential copyright issues may arise when students post their videos publicly online. Therefore, as Kessler and Marino (2023) remark, if teachers want to use YouTube or another public platform, then they need to teach their students how to find multimodal resources that are both free and publicly available for use. For instance, there are a number of online resources for finding stock images and video footage. Examples include Creative Commons, Mazwai and Pexels, all of which offer content that is copyright-free. Additionally, to avoid potential copyright issues, another possibility is that teachers could proactively set different restrictions as a means of keeping their students' content private. For example, if using YouTube to post students' digital video projects, teachers have the option of creating a private channel and adjusting the settings so that only specific people (i.e. the students and the teacher) have access to view the content. Thus, for obvious reasons, any copyright issue is a final important issue to consider, which comes at the conclusion of the composing process.

# 4 Outcomes and Evidence of Learning

**Introduction**

Apart from investigating second language (L2) learners' writing processes, as discussed in Chapter 3, perhaps the most critical area to be investigated thus far is digital multimodal composing (DMC) in relation to various *outcomes and evidence of learning*. After all, since the ultimate goal of most pedagogic activities is to help learners acquire the different linguistic forms and pragmatic competence they will need in order to communicate effectively, it is vital to understand the extent to which adopting DMC tasks are facilitative of such goals. Notably, research involving second language (L2) students' writing processes and learning outcomes has often been separated. This is for multiple reasons. For example, just because a learner is engaging in a certain type of composing behavior or process, this does not necessarily mean that he or she is adopting an appropriate or effective strategy. Relatedly, by engaging in a certain behavior or process, this also does not guarantee positive growth or development in terms of L2 learning outcomes. For such reasons, these two topics have also been separated into different chapters in this book.

In terms of the large body of research involving DMC, of the topics covered throughout this book (i.e. learners' writing processes, teachers' and students' perceptions and individual differences), investigations of outcomes and evidence of learning are the least robust. In fact, multiple scholars have noted the importance of expanding research agendas to understand the impacts of multimodal writing and DMC on L2 learning (e.g. Lim & Kessler, 2022; Manchón, 2017). (This topic is considered later in this chapter and also in Chapter 9.) Nevertheless, a number of studies speak to facets of DMC's effectiveness for promoting second language acquisition (SLA).

Thus, this chapter focuses on the topic of DMC's impact on L2 learning outcomes. Before venturing any further, it is important to define what is meant by *outcomes and evidence of learning*. In this chapter, primary emphasis is given to understanding L2 learning outcomes and/or development in terms of both the oral and written linguistic modes.

Particular attention is given to those areas identified by Polio (2017: 261), concerning 'change[s] over time in any of the following areas related to [oral or] written text production: language (e.g., complexity, accuracy, fluency, cohesion, mechanics); [and] knowledge of different genres...'. As part of Polio's definition, she also mentions 'metacognitive knowledge' and 'motivation'. However, these were intentionally omitted from the previous quote because discussions of these topics are provided in Chapter 6, which covers the area of DMC and individual differences. Importantly, although the oral and written linguistic modes are privileged throughout this chapter, outcomes and evidence of learning can also be understood as growth in a learner's capacity to understand and strategically manipulate other non-linguistic modes (e.g. using images or figures in a digital genre). In this chapter, however, linguistic modes are given prominence in an attempt to respond to some scholars' concerns about multimodal writing, particularly their fear that its use may stifle or impede linguistic development (e.g. Manchón, 2017; Qu, 2017).

When showcasing the body of literature that has investigated DMC-related outcomes and evidence of learning, this chapter divides research into two major categories or themes. These themes pertain to the methods that scholars have adopted in their research, which are broadly classified as (1) *studies adopting qualitative methods* and (2) *studies adopting quantitative or mixed methods.* In the other research-focused chapters of this book (i.e. Chapters 3, 5 and 6), four or five studies are presented that correspond to each theme. However, as noted, much of the research investigating DMC to date has been overwhelmingly qualitative in nature (also see reviews by Li and Akoto [2021] and Zhang *et al.* [2023]). Since much of the research discussed throughout this book is qualitative in scope, in this chapter, the focus is shifted by giving primary attention to theme 2 and studies that adopt quantitative or mixed methods. Like the other research-oriented chapters, all studies are discussed in considerable depth in an effort to highlight features of the studies, including their instructional contexts, DMC tasks/activities, research methods and results. Likewise, all studies are presented chronologically by date of publication (i.e. oldest to newest).

## Research: Key Findings

### Studies adopting qualitative methods

The first theme consists of studies that have used qualitative methods as a means of understanding the influence of DMC on various learning outcomes. When doing so, researchers have typically used data such as participant interviews and observations, in addition to collecting other artifacts (e.g. students' DMC projects, storyboards and written reflections). As is typical in qualitative studies, when presenting various learning outcomes, researchers have generally detailed specific instances or examples of L2 learning by highlighting aspects of individual learners' cases (e.g. reporting an insight gleaned from a participant observation).

One of the earliest DMC studies to fall into this qualitative methods category is Hepple *et al.* (2014). Although the authors never explicitly mention the term DMC in their article, it clearly falls within this realm. In their study, Hepple *et al.* (2014: 220) explored the general impact and affordances of a claymation video project, which refers to 'the process of stop-action filming clay figures'. The study took place in an intensive English language program in an Australian high school, which provided L2 English support for immigrant and refugee students. The focal course was a post-beginner class with 11 students. Interestingly, the claymation project arose after a class visit to a local art museum, which featured claymation videos that piqued students' interest. Because of this, their teacher subsequently created a claymation project, which centered around a pre-planned reading of a graded reader called *The Big Wave* (Buck, 1976), a story about life in Japan following a tsunami. The claymation video project consisted of multiple stages, including reading and analyzing the text, creating a storyboard, creating the clay models, writing the dialogue, filming the video, narrating the story, and editing and sharing the video. Thus, the claymation project required the use of multiple modes, such as images and video (of the clay figure), gestures (from the clay figure and other objects in the background), linguistic text (captions) and oral speech. The digital tools used for recording and editing the images and videos were not specified.

In implementing the project, the researchers (which included the classroom teacher) were motivated by multiliteracies (New London Group, 1996) primarily because their Australian curriculum also drew upon dimensions of the theoretical framework. Thus, the authors justified the project on such grounds, but they also noted that the project promoted diverse aspects of literacy, such as using contextually appropriate language, balancing speech and narration and requiring the use of a broad range of verb tenses. Hepple *et al.* (2014) focused on three focal participants called Jae-Sun, Egide and Semret, who worked together on the project. To investigate the affordances and learning outcomes, the authors collected the students' claymation videos and storyboards, took photos of different stages of the project and interviewed the students and the teacher. In the findings, Hepple *et al.* noted how the multi-stage nature of the project fostered collaborative relationships. For instance, the researchers detailed how the three students collaborated to discuss different modes (e.g. the spatial arrangement of design elements). Hepple *et al.* (2014: 227) also showcased how one of the more literate students (Jae-Sun) scaffolded his two partners, who had less developed writing abilities. Importantly, all three learners assumed 'expert' roles at different time points, each scaffolding their peers and contributing something to the project. Thus, Hepple *et al.*'s study reports on how the DMC project resulted in the learning of linguistic forms and content knowledge, particularly as a result of collective scaffolding.

In another early study, Lee (2014: 56) investigated the effects of repeated DMC activities on L2 English learners' writing skills and self-confidence. The researcher adopted a case study design to focus on two 'at-risk' English as a foreign language (EFL) writers with the pseudonyms Chen and Lin, whom the author noted struggled with linguistic and self-confidence issues. The study took place in an English program at a technological university in Taiwan, where the students had relatively low L2 proficiency. The researcher (also the teacher in the study) taught two English courses over two years, both of which focused on developing reading and writing skills. In one of the courses, Lee instituted a multi-part first-person narrative assignment, in which students discussed their general interests, friends and family, life experiences and more. Over the semester, students were required to complete five different narratives that included 10 sentences and photos, which had to be personally taken by the students. Learners then posted their narratives to a class discussion board for further comments and feedback from their peers. In the second course taught by the researcher, a digital storytelling project was implemented. This project was an expanded version of the first-person narrative activity from the first course, but this time, it required students to record a video and their voices. Unfortunately, the DMC tools used for each activity were not specified.

In terms of data collection, over the span of two years, Lee (2014) gathered the two students' DMC projects, discussion board postings, along with end-of-semester surveys in which the students reflected on the course and their L2 learning progress. Following data analysis, Lee also engaged in member checking as a means of understanding the participants' views of the findings. The students self-reported that they grew more confident in their abilities over time. For instance, in one of Lin's post-semester surveys, he stated that his confidence 'was low in the beginning', but he ultimately 'felt very satisfied' by the end of the course (Lee, 2014: 69). Most notably, the author highlighted both Chen's and Lin's L2 development over the two academic years. This was accomplished by highlighting the differences between one assignment (from Year 1) and another assignment (from Year 2). As illustrated in their projects, students' use of linguistic text and images became increasingly complex, as the learners began taking more risks in terms of playing with the language. Lee closed the study by highlighting DMC's capacity to serve as a foundational classroom activity, and its capacity to support at-risk students by providing them with different meaning-making resources.

The final qualitative study highlighted in this section is Tseng (2021). In her study, Tseng explored how four pre-service teachers in Taiwan engaged with DMC tasks, and how those tasks facilitated their acquisition of a written reflection genre. All four focal participants were upper-intermediate L2 English learners, who were enrolled in an elective professional writing class that provided academic literacy training. Similar to the other studies in this section, the researcher was the teacher of the class. As part of the 18-week course, Tseng taught reflective writing as an academic genre, and students completed different multimodal assignments throughout the semester, including slideshow presentations (with PowerPoint), digital posters and a video. The tools used for creating the posters and videos were not discussed. However, the researcher reported that students received explicit training in using multimedia tools. The teacher also covered how to integrate multiple modes to create different meanings.

In terms of data, Tseng (2021) collected students' DMC projects, reflection papers pertaining to the projects and post-study interviews in order to provide additional context. In her findings, Tseng reported that the use of the DMC tasks affected aspects of students' genre acquisition to varying degrees. Tseng (2021: 137) highlighted not only how some students transferred genre knowledge from their first language (L1), but also how the novel integration of different modes (e.g. images) made learning a 'dynamic' process which helped one learner better understand how to construct arguments. Another learner also stated that visualizing different aspects of language through images 'expanded my perspective of constructing arguments' (Tseng, 2021: 137). The learners were also highly capable of reproducing different elements of the target genre (e.g. the organizational structure). Finally, one participant noted that the DMC tasks facilitated her learning of the genre by providing her with 'more affordances to write the reflection genre' (Tseng, 2032: 139). Tseng closed the study by noting the capacity of DMC tasks to develop genre knowledge in the target language, which is a seldom-studied area in DMC scholarship.

## Studies adopting quantitative or mixed methods

The second theme showcased in this chapter pertains to studies that have investigated aspects of L2 learning outcomes by using quantitative or mixed methods. As mentioned in the introduction, most DMC literature to date has been qualitative in nature, relying on case studies that focus on either one or a small group of L2 learners. As such, in this chapter, more space is devoted to showcasing those exemplary quantitative or mixed methods studies in which researchers have used larger sample sizes and pursued experimental or quasi-experimental (i.e. classroom based) designs. Notably, of the small number of researchers who have adopted quantitative or mixed methods, most have tended to investigate L2 learning outcomes rather than other topics related to DMC such as writing processes or teachers' and students' perceptions.

Vandommele *et al.* (2017) is one such study, and it is perhaps the first study (to my knowledge) to employ quantitative methods. The authors noted that while previous research suggested potential benefits of adopting multimodal writing activities in the classroom, no studies had tested these assumptions using experimental methods. Therefore, the researchers sought not only to understand the effects of multimodal writing on L2 writing development, but also to investigate its effects when conducted in either in-school or out-of-school settings. The study took place with beginning learners of L2 Dutch in Belgium, who were between the ages of 12 and 18. A total of 84 students participated, and they were randomly assigned to one of three groups: an in-school group ($n = 26$), an out-of-school group ($n = 26$) or a non-intervention control group ($n = 32$). Both experimental groups (i.e. the in-school and out-of-school students) completed a multimodal writing assignment over two weeks. The DMC task required students to work collaboratively in groups to design a website that would introduce new arrivals and visitors to Flanders, a region in Belgium. Although students received training, the specific tools and platforms used for creating the websites were not explicitly mentioned.

To assess L2 learning outcomes, Vandommele *et al.* (2017) used a pretest (a narrative writing task) and a posttest (a persuasive task). While doing so, they focused solely on features of the linguistic written form in terms of students' improvement from pretest to posttest. Features included communicative effectiveness (rated holistically on a 7-item scale), lexical diversity (i.e. the range of vocabulary items used), syntactic complexity measures (e.g. mean length of T-unit, clauses per T-unit), accuracy (e.g. error-free T-units) and text length (i.e. total number of words produced). For those measures that required reliability coding (e.g. holistic quality), the researchers obtained and reported inter-rater reliability. To analyze their data and compare the outcomes for the three groups, the researchers used multilevel modeling (see their article for a description and justification). In terms of linguistic writing development, Vandommele *et al.* reported that both experimental groups (in and out of school) showed growth compared to the control group. Both experimental groups performed similarly, but they each outperformed the control group on measures of syntactic complexity and text length, among others. In closing, the researchers noted the potential of DMC tasks in both in-school and out-of-school contexts, particularly as a means of promoting beginning L2 learners' writing development.

Another early study is Dzekoe (2017), in which the author adopted mixed methods to investigate aspects of L2 learning outcomes with DMC. In his study, Dzekoe investigated L2 English learners' self-revision behaviors when engaging in a series of DMC tasks, and specifically, how students' revision behaviors in those tasks facilitated their conscious noticing of different linguistic items (drawing on Schmidt's 1990 noticing hypothesis). The study took place in an undergraduate ESL writing course in the United States, in which the researcher also served as the course instructor. During the semester, 22 students wrote an expository essay using Google Docs, which required them to discuss their role model and the impact that person had on their life. After writing the essay, students then transformed their essays into an online digital poster using the multimedia platform Glogster. Following the Google Docs and Glogster activities, students completed other post-activities including a reflection paper and a listening activity with the tool NaturalReader. Students inputted their essays into the online software NaturalReader, which read their texts back to them aloud. This was done to help promote noticing and to help students revise their essays for grammar and style.

Dzekoe (2017) collected a large amount of data, including surveys, students' revision histories on Google Docs, their online posters and written reflections, and also stimulated recalls, in which students were prompted to discuss how/why they edited their multimodal posters. All 22 students' data were included in the quantitative portion of the study, but for the qualitative portion, an in-depth analysis of six students' data was presented. Dzekoe (2017: 78) coded the data for 'observable behavior of [students'] noticing', which included revisions they made such as additions, deletions and substitutions. The data were coded by both the researcher and a second coder in order to obtain inter-coder reliability (90% agreement). Dzekoe then used a $t$-test to compare the total number of revisions made by students in each assignment. In the results, students reported that the use of multiple modes enabled them to communicate more effectively than through text alone. When the Google Docs activity was combined with the NaturalReader listening activity, 86% of the students stated that they felt it prompted noticing. The quantitative data supported some of the qualitative comments made by students, as learners progressively engaged in more revisions when moving between assignments. A $t$-test also indicated a statistically significant difference in the number of revisions between some of the assignments. Dzekoe concluded by noting the pedagogical implications of his study in terms of transforming traditional essay tasks into DMC projects to promote L2 learners' noticing and audience awareness.

The next study is Kim and Belcher (2020), in which the researchers explored the extent to which DMC tasks compared to traditional monomodal argumentative essays. This study was motivated in part by multiliteracies (New London Group, 1996), and also by criticisms discussed earlier in this chapter, in which scholars have questioned the utility of DMC and its capacity to promote linguistic development (e.g. Qu, 2017). As such, Kim and Belcher conducted an exploratory study, recruiting 18 L2 English learners who were enrolled in a university-level writing course in South Korea. The learners were assigned both a traditional essay and a DMC project as homework outside of class, and they were given one month to complete them. The writing prompt involved applying for a job where applicants (i.e. the students) had to complete two tasks: (1) to compose a traditional argumentative essay on a topic of their choosing and (2) to create a DMC project on that same topic. For the DMC project, students were required to storyboard for planning purposes and to write a script for oral narration. The DMC task appeared to be left open to students, as it was not clearly specified. However, when completing the tasks, the authors adopted a within-group design, meaning that all learners completed both tasks. The order of the tasks was counterbalanced to avoid practice or ordering effects.

In addition to collecting students' argumentative essays and DMC projects, Kim and Belcher (2020) collected project reflection journals and a post-study survey that assessed students' perspectives of the two tasks (discussed in Chapter 5). The researchers then analyzed students' DMC oral narration scripts and argumentative essays for measures of syntactic complexity (number of words per T-unit, number of clauses per T-unit) and accuracy (accurate clauses/total number of clauses). Inter-coder reliability was not reported. Afterward, three paired samples *t*-tests were used to search for differences between the two compositions. In their results, Kim and Belcher reported that the traditional essay was more syntactically complex with a small to medium effect size. However, there were no significant differences between the two compositions in terms of accuracy. These findings differ from those of Vandommele *et al.* (2017). Kim and Belcher (2020: 96) noted that these conflicting findings could be due to differences in the two studies' designs, and also because the oral speech script used in their study likely elicited informal and 'less academic' speech compared to the academic nature of the argumentative essay. (This is a potential design issue, which I return to in the next section when discussing implications for researchers).

In another study by Yang *et al.* (2020), the researchers examined the effectiveness of a digital storytelling task on L2 English learners' speaking skills and creative thinking. Their study was motivated by interactionist approaches, and specifically, Swain's (1985, 1993) output hypothesis. Creative thinking was defined as 'higher order thinking' and students' capacity 'to critically generate ideas' (see Andiliou & Murphy, 2010: 217). In the study, Yang *et al.* (2020) adopted a quasi-experimental design with 54 participants in Taiwan who were in two seventh-grade classes (ages 14–15). The same teacher taught both classes, and one class ($n = 27$) received a traditional present-practice-produce (PPP) form of instruction, while the second class ($n = 27$) received instruction that was based around a multi-week digital storytelling task. The researchers stated that the two groups were equivalent based on factors such as age, gender and years of English learning experience, but no specific numerical data were provided. The study lasted eight weeks, and the digital storytelling group completed a project about career planning. For the project, students who shared similar career goals worked together in groups of four. The teacher spent approximately 50% of each class pre-teaching content, grammar and vocabulary, and students spent the remainder of class time working on their project. Each week, students completed a sequence of activities that built toward the final project, including brainstorming story ideas (Week 1), selecting their topics (Week 2), creating storyboards (Week 3), writing scripts (Week 4), revising the scripts (Week 5), assembling the stories (Week 6), revising the stories (Week 7) and presenting their final projects (Week 8). Students received training with multimedia tools, including Prezi (for presentations), Audacity (for audio recording) and Inspiration (for content mapping). The PPP group was taught the same content, grammar and vocabulary; however, instead of the digital storytelling project, they engaged in textbook exercises, reading exercises and speaking drills.

Yang *et al.* (2020) adopted a pretest-posttest design to assess both groups' development of speaking skills and creative thinking. The speaking test consisted of 21 items, and for creative thinking, the researchers' adopted the *Torrance Tests of Creative Thinking* (see Torrance, 1998), which assessed the three constructs of fluency, flexibility and originality. The researchers then ran an analysis of variance (ANCOVA) and multivariate analysis of variance (MANCOVA) for statistical comparisons. The results of the study showed that the group who participated in the digital storytelling project received significantly higher scores in terms of oral fluency and accuracy, with a large effect size. These results also held true for the creative thinking posttest results for all subscales. Thus, the researchers noted that their study was one of the first to look at DMC tasks and their effects on oral production. They also noted the pedagogical utility of adopting such collaborative tasks for prompting L2 output and higher-order thinking skills.

While Yang *et al.* (2020) explored DMC's impact on learners' oral skills, Cho and Kim (2021) conducted a mixed methods study that investigated DMC's influence on writing skills. Their study took place in a South Korean high school with a group of 31 intermediate-level L2 English learners. Cho and Kim were motivated by multiliteracies (New London Group, 1996), and they were specifically interested in understanding the affordances of DMC compared to traditional monomodal tasks. Therefore, all 31 students engaged in both tasks, including a monomodal summary reflection essay and a DMC summary reflection task. The students first read a short graded reader (a fable of 372 words). They were then given a prompt and told to 'imagine you are participating in a summary-reflection essay contest' that required students to submit 'a traditional monomodal essay and a digital multimodal composition to be uploaded to YouTube' (Cho & Kim, 2021: 9). For the DMC project, the students were instructed to use the free video-editing software Adobe Spark Video. Before engaging in the DMC task, the teacher showed the students example videos and encouraged them to integrate different modes. Students were given two class sessions to complete the monomodal task and five class sessions to create their digital videos. To minimize any potential practice effects, the researchers counterbalanced the order of tasks with one half of the students completing the monomodal task first.

Once students had finished both compositions, they were scored using an analytic rubric (adapted from Plakans & Gebril, 2015) that accounted for areas including content, organization and language use. Inter-rater reliability was obtained by having two raters independently assess 50% of the dataset, with high reliability reported for both the DMC task ($r = 0.91$) and the monomodal essay ($r = 0.89$). In their results, Cho and Kim (2021) reported that there were no statistically significant differences in any of the three categories. The researchers also presented data from two case study participants to highlight their findings, showing how students successfully produced summary reflections in both conditions, for instance, by using 'complex grammatical structures with a high level of accuracy' (Cho & Kim, 2021: 14). They also illustrated how the two students expressed the same ideas in the monomodal text compared to the digital video (e.g. by using images, oral narration, text and background music). Cho and Kim closed their study by noting that their results suggest that, contrary to some scholars' concerns, students' literacy, reasoning and writing skills do not appear to be sacrificed when engaging in DMC.

Xu (2021) is the final study presented in this section, in which the researcher examined the effects of DMC on writing performance. Specifically, Xu used a quantitative-only design that examined the impact of repeated DMC projects on L2 English learners' writing development. The study took place at a Chinese university with 96 participants, who were drawn from three sections of an undergraduate course called 'College English' (Xu, 2021: 6). One teacher taught the course. A placement test (not specified) indicated that students were intermediate-level speakers of L2 English. Using a pretest-posttest design, all participants in the three course sections completed two monomodal argumentative writing tasks before and after the treatment. Following the pretest, two class sections were assigned to the experimental group ($n = 66$) and one class was assigned to the control group ($n = 30$). The experimental classes worked in groups of four or five over an academic semester to complete three different DMC projects. The projects were labeled as digital videos, although the scope of the projects and tools was somewhat unclear. All three projects required students to go through different stages, including reading texts, discussing ideas, writing scripts and creating/editing videos. The three topics included (1) technology and relationships, (2) the role of universities in society and (3) the role of punishment in education. The control group received instruction on the same topics; however, they completed monomodal essays instead of DMCs.

To assess students' writing development over the semester, Xu (2021) analyzed the pretests and posttests for both linguistic and functional aspects. This consisted of numerous measures of complexity, accuracy and fluency, in addition to areas such as content, task requirement, comprehensibility and cohesion. All holistic measures were adapted from a scale created by Kuiken and Vedder (2017). When scoring the texts, Xu reported high inter-rater reliability for 10% of the dataset ($\alpha = 0.86$). A series of mixed ANOVAs were then used to analyze the measures of L2 writing performance. In the results, Xu reported that the experimental DMC group showed significant improvement in multiple areas compared to the control group. Those areas included syntactic complexity (mean length of T-unit), content, comprehensibility and fluency (text length), with a large effect size found for fluency. No differences were detected for any of the accuracy measures (e.g. error-free clauses, error-free T-units). The author noted that many of the findings are comparable to Vandommele et al. (2017). In terms of explaining the developmental differences between the experimental and control groups, Xu remarked that the experimental group worked collaboratively (composed of four or five students per group), which possibly afforded additional opportunities for interaction and peer-to-peer scaffolding. Therefore, future research may be needed that explores individuals' use of DMC.

## Implications for Researchers

Based on a review of the literature in the previous section, the focus now shifts to a discussion of the implications. In particular, this section discusses important takeaways for researchers, including notes about the previous studies' methods, the need for future scholarship and the need for more comprehensive and transparent reporting in published studies.

In terms of the studies exploring DMC in relation to outcomes and evidence of learning, from a researcher's perspective, what is clear is that there is a general need for more quantitative and mixed methods studies. This is important because the goal of qualitative studies is not to generalize findings, but rather to understand the situated nature of individuals who are embedded within specific instructional contexts, or as De Costa et al. (2022: 427) have noted, to have readers understand 'how sociocultural and socioeconomic conditions impact language learning and teaching'. Therefore, quantitative and mixed methods studies are needed to help researchers understand the broader, more generalizable effects of DMC.

Of the quantitative and mixed methods studies reviewed in this chapter, the only study that did not appear to show any advantages for DMC compared to traditional monomodal tasks was Kim and Belcher (2020). In their study, Kim and Belcher found that the traditional essay was more syntactically complex with a small to medium effect size. These findings differ from other studies, which show either no differences (e.g. Cho & Kim, 2021) or a greater influence for DMC on syntactic complexity measures when compared to monomodal writing (e.g. Vandommele *et al.*, 2017; Xu, 2021). However, Kim and Belcher's study has a potential issue in its design and subsequent interpretation, which may have led to this finding. In the analysis stage, the authors compared students' monomodal essays to the same students' DMC projects. However, the DMC project that they used for the analysis was a script, which was written for oral narration purposes. Based on their study, it appears that their students wrote the oral script first, with no other modes integrated. Therefore, it can be argued that the researchers are not truly comparing a DMC project to a monomodal essay. Instead, what they are actually doing is making a one-to-one mode comparison by using text in a script that does not attempt to leverage other modes. What Kim and Belcher's (2020) study appears to be comparing then is different *registers* or, in this case, oral speech versus academic writing. The authors even make explicit reference to this potential limitation in the discussion section of their paper. Therefore, since the researchers are ultimately comparing oral speech with academic writing, it is not surprising that they found students' academic writing (in the monomodal essay) to be more syntactically complex. Other writing researchers have also noted this to be the case, even calling for different complexity measures to assess oral and written registers, respectively (e.g. Biber *et al.*, 2011; Kuiken *et al.*, 2019).

The studies reviewed in this chapter appear to suggest that there are distinct advantages for DMC in terms of its influence on various measures of complexity, accuracy and fluency. However, a key question subsequently arises from these results. A simple (yet perhaps not so simple) question is: *Why?* That is, if these results hold true for additional studies in the future, why is it that DMC is impacting learning in this way? This is something that is not truly understood. As such, future researchers interested in DMC's effects might consider exploring this further. Relatedly, as readers will note, many of the quantitative and mixed methods studies outlined in this chapter use relatively traditional means-based tests (e.g. $t$-tests, ANOVAs) for comparison purposes. Because of the inherent limitations in these types of statistical tests, future studies are needed that adopt more nuanced and advanced statistical techniques such as multiple regression (see Larson-Hall, 2016; Plonsky & Ghanbar, 2018). For instance, future research is needed to examine what factors are contributing to these learning gains. As discussed in Chapter 6 on individual differences, it is possible that various individual differences (e.g. motivation, metacognition and identity) play unique, meaningful roles in students' engagement with DMC. Therefore, it is possible that the confluence of some factors (i.e. increased motivation and metacognition) from DMC may account for a significant portion (or variance explained) in terms of why development is spurred more so compared to that of traditional monomodal essay tasks.

Unfortunately, it is also a distinct possibility that another factor is at play here. Some of the DMC studies that focus on learning outcomes accidentally appear to have introduced a confounding variable, which has the potential to adversely affect the results. This pertains to the use of individual versus collaborative writing activities in the studies' designs. For instance, in Xu (2021: 8), the researcher noted that the control group had some 'opportunities to collaborate and interact with peers', yet it seems that this control group also engaged in much more solitary work (e.g. by writing individual essays and receiving written feedback from their teacher only). Conversely, the experimental DMC groups in the study worked collaboratively with four or five peers over the span of an entire academic semester to complete their projects. These differences in peer-to-peer interaction have the potential to be a major issue. This is because studies of collaborative writing have shown that those who engage in repeated collaborative writing activities are more likely to outperform their peers who write individually, based on posttests that examine individual writing gains (e.g. Bikowski & Vithanage, 2016). Because of this, future researchers need to be extremely careful when designing their studies to make sure that (a) the control and experimental groups spend the same amount of time working in pairs/groups, or that (b) both the DMC and monomodal tasks are assigned as individual tasks only.

Like Chapter 3, which covered learners' DMC writing processes, when it comes to research investigating outcomes and evidence of learning, there is also a real need for more longitudinal studies. There are two exceptions in this chapter: Lee (2014) and Xu (2021). Lee's study is impressive in that it tracked learners over the span of two years, but Xu's study is also commendable in that it investigated learning outcomes following a full semester of instruction. Still, these are rarities among studies of any methodological approach (i.e. qualitative, quantitative or mixed methods). Methodologically speaking, qualitative studies that follow learners for (at least) one semester or longer are perhaps more plausible in terms of their execution. Therefore, qualitative studies are needed that track the same learners over time, understand how those learners engage with specific and/or different DMC tasks and genres and analyze how students' experiences with those genres impact their learning over time. In terms of quantitative or mixed methods studies, future research is needed that adopts quasi-experimental designs similar to Xu (2021), in which classrooms of students receive the same instruction yet engage in either monomodal or multimodal writing tasks, respectively.

The final topic discussed in this section on research implications again pertains to future scholarship; however, it is not a research direction *per se*. Of the studies reviewed in this chapter, readers may have noticed that when it came to reporting on the studies' methods and procedures, I frequently resorted to saying something similar to 'The tools used for X project were not discussed'. When reviewing studies for this chapter, often I noted that the full scope of the DMC project used in the study was unclear. Sometimes, this pertained to the steps involved in students completing the DMC task. Most often though, this lack of clarity or specificity involved researchers not reporting the digital tools, software or platforms they used. This is an issue for a number of reasons. Most notably, for those researchers who wish to conduct different types of replication studies in the future (see Porte, 2012; Porte & McManus, 2018), this makes doing so considerably more challenging, as they will then need to attempt to track down the original authors and contact them in order to obtain this information. Pedagogically, too, knowing the specific software or tools that were used in a study is one of the most critical pieces of information that pre-service and in-service teachers may wish to know. Without this information, teachers may get a general sense of the stages of the DMC project and how to structure them, but they may be left wondering what tools to use when doing so (see Chapter 7 on DMC tasks and activities for an extended discussion). Therefore, when publishing work in the future, researchers must be clear and transparent when reporting this information.

**Implications for Teachers**

The final section of this chapter now moves to a more focused discussion of the classroom implications. Drawing on the findings of the studies outlined in this chapter, three pedagogical implications for practitioners pertaining to outcomes and evidence of learning are discussed.

The first implication comes from Dzekoe (2017). In the study, the researcher had students transform a traditional monomodal assignment (i.e. an essay) into a new DMC genre (a digital poster using Glogster), which was subsequently followed up by a listening activity with the online tool NaturalReader. The sequencing of these activities in the study is noteworthy in that students first had the opportunity to practice a more traditional test-oriented genre. This may be important for teachers to assign, especially in some contexts where students need to prepare for a standardized proficiency test such as the International English Language Testing System (IELTS) or the Test of English as a Foreign Language (TOEFL). However, this does not mean that students must *only* practice test-oriented essay genres. Since digital posters are a multimodal genre that many students may have to produce at some point in their academic programs (see Lim & Polio, 2020), it may be important to teach students this genre as well. Thus, having students engage with a digital poster task may be both authentic and meaningful based on students' future needs. Importantly, too, is that by sequencing the tasks in this way (i.e. moving from a monomodal essay to a multimodal genre) may raise students' awareness of features of the audience and help promote conscious noticing of other linguistic forms as students attempt to transform their writing into something that is more appropriate for a poster. Finally, it is worth noting that NaturalReader is a free and easy-to-use tool, so this is something that teachers may wish to use with their students and/or make them aware of. As noted in Dzekoe's study, tools such as NaturalReader can be particularly helpful for students, since hearing their writing in another (oral) mode may help them notice a myriad of issues.

The second pedagogical implication pertains to DMC's impact on various skills. Some teachers may be worried that since 'composition' is in the title of the term DMC, it is therefore a writing activity that is only applicable to a writing classroom. However, of the studies reviewed in this chapter, the findings suggest that collaborative DMC tasks have the capacity not only to positively influence students' writing skills (e.g. Vandommele *et al.*, 2017), but also to impact other areas such as learners' oral production and creative thinking (e.g. Yang *et al.*, 2020). For teachers in integrated skills classes (i.e. classes that focus on developing reading, writing, speaking and listening skills), this is important to note. If a DMC activity is implemented strategically, it can help L2 learners with multiple skills. As other studies have shown, too, it is both possible and relatively easy to integrate reading tasks with DMC. For instance, Hepple *et al.* (2014) first had their students read a short graded reader, which then served as the foundation for creating the DMC project that followed. When teachers get creative in this way, they can develop a DMC task that leverages an assigned reading or required text, and then use this as a means for working on other skills such as writing and speaking (and listening, if a post-activity is implemented in which students have to present or share their projects).

The third and final pedagogical implication from this chapter is somewhat related to the previous one. This has to do with DMC being implemented as a multi-stage project. As discussed in Chapter 5, which covers teachers' and students' perceptions, teachers have sometimes voiced concerns about adopting DMC tasks. One major concern is that some feel that DMC tasks take a considerable amount of time when it comes to setting up the project, training students to use the necessary digital tools and then giving their students enough class time to actually finish the task. A solution to this problem can be found in a number of studies discussed in this chapter. For instance, in Vandommele *et al.* (2017), the authors had one group of students create their projects (websites) as an out-of-school homework activity. Importantly, the benefits of implementing this task out of school appeared to mirror those of the students who completed their websites in school.

Another alternative is showcased in Yang *et al.* (2020), who implemented the tasks in class. In the study, the teacher assigned a DMC task (digital storytelling) as a multi-stage project. During a portion of one academic semester, the teacher had students complete a sequence of activities that culminated in a final digital storytelling project. This included brainstorming (Week 1), selecting topics (Week 2), storyboarding (Week 3), writing scripts (Week 4), revising scripts (Week 5), assembling stories (Week 6), revising stories (Week 7) and finally, having students present their projects (Week 8). This seems to be a particularly effective means of taking on an otherwise time-consuming project. That is, instead of devoting full or consecutive days to working on the digital storytelling project, the teacher turned it into a multi-stage project. By cutting it up into smaller chunks, this made it more manageable for both the teacher and the students. Therefore, if teachers are potentially concerned about the time-on-task factor and whether it will detract from other aspects of their curriculum, they may wish to consider assigning DMC as either an out-of-class activity or implementing it as a multi-stage project that spans multiple weeks.

# 5 Teachers' and Students' Perceptions

**Introduction**

This chapter turns to a discussion of research that has investigated *teachers' and students' perceptions* of digital multimodal composing (DMC). In the fields of applied linguistics, education and second language acquisition (SLA), scholarship examining aspects of teachers' and learners' beliefs, thoughts and perceptions has long been a staple of academic work. Most pertinent to this chapter, such investigations have been especially widespread throughout various subdisciplines such as computer-assisted language learning (CALL; e.g. Kessler, 2021b; Lawrence, 2014), educational technology (e.g. Fidalgo *et al.*, 2020; Palak & Walls, 2014) and second language (L2) writing (e.g. Mao & Crosthwaite, 2019; Shehadeh, 2011; Zhang, 2020). Broadly speaking, studies that focus on different stakeholders' beliefs have often been justified by a handful of rationales. For instance, in terms of gauging teachers' perceptions of adopting different CALL-based tools and activities, Lawrence (2018) has noted that in an increasingly digital world, it is imperative to understand educators' beliefs about the affordances and drawbacks of different technologies for the L2 classroom. Similarly, it is also important to understand the vantage points of students. As Sydorenko *et al.* (2017) have commented, by comprehending students' beliefs about different digital tools, teachers are more likely to empathize with their students, and they are also more likely to encourage buy-in when attempting to integrate CALL activities into their classrooms.

Another rationale for investigating teachers' and students' perceptions pertains to potential differences between these two groups. Namely, a number of studies have shown that students' viewpoints do not always align with those of their instructors', and particularly so when it comes to topics involving teachers' and students' perceptions of the effectiveness of different tasks, along with how enjoyable learners find them to be (e.g. Ahmadian *et al.*, 2017; Murphy, 2003). Research has also suggested that many teachers and researchers may have a tendency to take L2 learners' beliefs and practices for granted. For example, studies such as Kessler *et al.* (2020b) have illustrated that language teachers may have serious misconceptions about how often their L2 learners engage with the target language beyond the classroom. Additionally, other studies have suggested that instructors may have misconceptions regarding their students' technological literacy, access and general interest in engaging in CALL (e.g. Winke & Goertler, 2008). For these reasons and more, scholars who are interested in fostering connections between theory, research and practice have found it necessary to understand both teachers' and learners' perceptions, especially around issues concerning technology use.

This chapter focuses on the topic of *teachers' and students' perceptions* of various DMC tasks and activities when implemented in a myriad of instructional settings. When highlighting the literature that has investigated teachers' and/or students' perceptions, this chapter segments research into three major categories or themes. Somewhat predictably, these themes are broadly classified here as (1) *studies of teachers' perceptions*, (2) *studies of students' perceptions* and (3) *studies comparing teachers' and students' perceptions*. In the previous research-focused chapters (i.e. Chapters 3 and 4), four or five studies corresponding to each theme were presented. However, although there are an abundance of studies that focus on themes 1 and 2, there are few existing studies for theme 3, which directly compares and contrasts the perceptions of teachers and their students. Therefore, only two studies are discussed in relation to theme 3. For all themes, individual studies are described in depth as a means of highlighting design features, including the different student populations, focal DMC tasks and the studies' results. For each theme, studies are presented chronologically by date of publication (i.e. oldest to newest).

## Research: Key Findings

### Studies of teachers' perceptions

The first theme consists of studies that have examined the implementation or use of DMC tasks from the perspectives of teachers. In applied linguistics and SLA, when people have implemented either a new pedagogical approach (e.g. task-based language teaching) or a new classroom activity, often one of the first types of studies conducted is an investigation of instructors' perspectives (e.g. Carless, 2007; Chen & Wright, 2017). Often, such studies tend to be qualitative in nature, in which researchers adopt semi-structured interviews or other ethnographic methods such as observations. In these perception-oriented studies, researchers often attempt to gauge issues such as teachers' thoughts about the relative ease or difficulty of implementing the approach or activity, how it generally compares to their current practices, whether it conflicts with school-driven curricula or testing goals and more. With DMC, such topics have also been investigated, as teachers have attempted to implement different DMC tasks and activities in their respective classrooms.

One of the first studies in this area is Ryu and Boggs (2016). In their study, which was motivated by multiliteracies (New London Group, 1996), the authors explored how English language teachers in South Korea perceived the integration of multimodal writing activities into their classrooms. Ryu and Boggs (2016: 54) were particularly interested in understanding the perceptions of those teachers who actively adopted DMC, especially since the target instructional context, as they stated, often 'privilege[ed] above all, standardized test scores'. Five teachers were recruited to participate in the study, and these teachers indicated that they adopted some form of multimodal composition in their pedagogies. One teacher worked in a middle school, while the other four teachers worked in a high school setting. In order to understand the teachers' perceptions and to triangulate their findings, Ryu and Boggs collected data in the form of surveys and classroom artifacts, and they also conducted semi-structured interviews and classroom observations.

In their findings, Ryu and Boggs (2016) stated that as part of their general pedagogical practices, the focal participants regularly adopted multimodal sources of input (e.g. images and video). These teachers did so because, based on their experiences, they felt it motivated their students to write more as opposed to solely relying on traditional linguistic-based text exercises. Interestingly, all five teachers reportedly adopted multimodal composition activities for pre-writing or post-reading purposes. For instance, in order to help students learn English vocabulary, one teacher regularly had students use movie-making software to create 'vocabulary video clips' (Ryu & Boggs, 2016: 56). In order to help students understand the stories they had read, another teacher had students produce digital illustrated books that covered different aspects of the focal story's characters, themes, settings and more. All five teachers clearly had positive perceptions about multimodality in general, and particularly, the influence of different modes on students' motivation and their ability to learn the target language. Notably, however, the fact that all five teachers had such positive perceptions can be attributed to the fact that the researchers purposefully sampled from teachers who had already adopted DMC. Nevertheless, it is interesting to note how these five teachers adopted DMC in various ways in a test-heavy context.

Similar to Ryu and Boggs (2016), Tan and Matsuda (2020) were motivated by multiliteracies (New London Group, 1996). In their study of teachers' perceptions, Tan and Matsuda (2020: 2) opened their article with a discussion of how (at the time) little was known about 'how multimodal writing pedagogy is implemented, or whether it is implemented at all'; the authors also noted that to date, much of DMC's use appeared to 'depend on the individual's decision and personal impetus to do so'. Therefore, Tan and Matsuda explored nine English language teachers' beliefs about integrating multimodality into their practice and what internal and external factors influenced their beliefs about multimodal writing. All nine teachers in the study were graduate teaching assistants who taught first-year, university-level composition courses in the United States. The participants had between one and two years of teaching experience, and they were currently enrolled in different doctoral programs at the researchers' university (e.g. applied linguistics, English literature).

To investigate the focal teachers' beliefs, the researchers collected a combination of online surveys, interviews and artifacts such as the participants' teaching materials. Similar to Ryu and Boggs' (2016) findings, Tan and Matsuda (2020) reported that the graduate teaching assistants gave either medium or high priority to integrating multimodal assignments into their courses, and the participants felt that such assignments were particularly important in today's society. However, the teachers did have rather different pedagogical agendas in mind. For instance, some teachers tended to focus more on *modal complexity*, in which their primary goal was to help their learners comprehend the affordances of non-linguistic modes. Other teachers were more focused on *critical analysis*, or helping students develop their critical reading skills. Finally, some teachers tended to focus more on leveraging DMC for developing students' *subject-matter knowledge* or fostering *rhetorical awareness*. When asked about their students, most teachers agreed that their learners were highly proficient technology users; however, two teachers expressed concerns about international students' abilities to perform multimodal tasks when compared to their domestic student peers. Tan and Matsuda also reported that the teachers' practices were most affected by their perceptions of their students, along with their confidence and knowledge of multimodal literacy in general.

Li (2020) is another teacher perception study driven by multiliteracies, which investigated graduate student assistants' perspectives on integrating multimodal writing practices into the curriculum. Data from Li's study came from a larger project that explored the implementation of multimodal projects in her graduate program's Teaching English to Speakers of Other Languages (TESOL)/applied linguistics curriculum. For her study, Li integrated DMC projects into two online TESOL graduate courses that she taught (titled General Linguistics and TESOL Methods). Students were recruited after the courses had concluded, and in total, nine pre-service and in-service student-teachers agreed to participate. In terms of the DMC tasks, one project required the teachers in-training to create a reflection that synthesized the knowledge they had gained during the class; the other project required participants to design multimodal instructional materials for a target English as a second language/English as a foreign language (ESL/EFL) context of their choice. The teachers were given a range of software and tools to develop their projects, including Glogster, PowerPoint, Powtoon, Prezi, Storybird,

Vyond and WeVideo. However, Li noted that students did not receive any explicit training with these tools. Li also created rubrics to assess both projects, and the rubrics included areas for grading content, creativity, graphic design, language and mechanics, and technology use.

For data analysis, Li (2020) collected the participants' multimodal projects, and she also gauged their perceptions by conducting semi-structured interviews and collecting written narratives, in which participants recounted their thoughts and experiences while working on their projects. After analyzing the data, Li reported that the pre-/in-service teachers had favorable perceptions of the DMC projects. Some participants noted that they felt it deepened their engagement with the class content and 'integrated all the levels of skills... particularly the higher cognitive skills' (Li, 2020: 7). Some participants also stated that experiencing the project as a student fostered their motivation to use similar DMC projects in their own classrooms in the future. Despite their positivity, some participants reported multiple challenges when engaging with the projects. For example, because the projects were relatively open-ended, some struggled with topic selection and found it to be somewhat 'daunting at first' (Li, 2020: 8). Additionally, other students struggled due to their unfamiliarity with the technology platforms, in addition to completing the DMC project in the requested timeframe. Thus, Li's study is noteworthy in that it engages pre-/in-service teachers in DMC from a student's vantage point, and it also helps teachers understand the potential benefits and drawbacks of implementing similar projects in their own classrooms.

For the final study in this section, Normann (2022) investigated a similar pre-service teacher population. However, Normann was interested in examining teachers' perspectives as they engaged in a digital storytelling task for L2 English teaching purposes. Participants in the study were enrolled in a master's teacher training program in English language education, and data collection coincided with a training workshop that focused on digital storytelling. In the workshop, the pre-service teachers were required to create their own digital stories for teaching English. Participants were provided with a prompt, which asked them to develop a short script and a digital story with images and personal narration. Their digital stories were to be based on a young adult novel called *My Brother's Name is Jessica* (Boyne, 2019). To complete the digital storytelling task, the pre-service teachers were given two options: (1) tell a story or share reflections from the perspective of one of the book's characters or (2) recount their own experiences of reading all or parts of the book. Afterward, all of the participants wrote reflection papers on their experiences with creating their digital stories. The tools used for creating the digital stories were not specified.

Following an analysis of the pre-service teachers' reflection papers, Normann (2022) reported some of the successes and challenges that the participants faced when engaging in the task. After writing the story, some participants found it challenging to find pictures on the internet, so they ended up drawing their own because they found this to be faster. However, the pre-service teachers also noted that the images afforded opportunities for meaning making that were not represented in their written texts. Specifically, one participant stated that 'suddenly I had to express the emotions that was [sic] not expressed with words, and the story gets even more depth. This also kind of make [sic] you understand the novel a bit more as well' (Normann, 2022: 196). Thus, similar to Li's (2020) study, Normann's findings are of interest because they shed light on some of the non-linguistic affordances of digital storytelling while also highlighting the challenges that teachers might encounter with this task in their own classrooms.

## Studies of students' perceptions

The second theme consists of studies that have examined the use of DMC tasks from students' perspectives. Similar to research that has investigated teachers' perceptions, studies of students' perceptions have traditionally been qualitative in nature, although there has been the occasional exception (e.g. Chen [2018], which is described further in what follows). In studies of students' perceptions, researchers – who are often the teachers of the focal classrooms as well – have attempted to understand learners' beliefs about the effectiveness of different DMC activities, how enjoyable students find those activities to be and what general affordances and drawbacks students feel they possess, among other areas.

One early study of L2 learners' perceptions of DMC is Castañeda (2013). In her study, the researcher examined students' overall opinions of a digital storytelling task that was integrated into a high school L2 Spanish curriculum in the United States. A total of 12 participants took part in the case study. The digital storytelling task itself took 12 weeks and consisted of multiple stages, such as 'brainstorming, scripting, giving and receiving feedback, revising scripts, designing storyboards, recording audio, and digitizing the story elements' (Castañeda, 2013: 50). Since many students in the class were preparing to graduate from high school, the prompt for the project asked the students to recount a high school experience and to share it with their peers and teachers. The final stage of the project involved students showcasing their digital stories in a movie premiere event. To create their stories, students gathered photos from their personal archives and social media accounts (e.g. Facebook), and then edited their stories using iMovie.

To understand students' perspectives of the digital storytelling task, Castañeda (2013) collected multiple sources of data, including questionnaires (both pre- and post-project), focus group discussions (pre- and post-project) and observations and reflection journals, which were kept by the classroom teacher and the researcher. In her findings, Castañeda reported students' perceptions both at the pre-project and post-project phases. Pre-project, most students appeared to understand the task, and they were more concerned with L2 Spanish language issues, such as how to formulate the appropriate grammar in order to complete the task. However, some students expressed anxiety about having to use the iMovie software, as one student remarked that using Mac computers was generally 'confusing' (Castañeda, 2013: 52). During the process of creating their digital stories, students particularly enjoyed being able to review and edit their work, stating that it enabled them to catch their mistakes and increase their own self-awareness of language issues. Post-project, most students stated that they enjoyed the task, but one student felt that the task could be improved by enabling learners to interact with each other more.

Similar to Castañeda's (2013) study, Chen (2018) also investigated students' perceptions of a specific DMC task, although in Chen's article, she examined students' perceptions of a digital video project. Chen's study took place at a university in Taiwan with 46 students who were enrolled in a required EFL course called Freshman English. Students ranged in L2 English proficiency from lower intermediate to advanced. As part of the course, a digital video project was assigned, which apart from developing the learners' English skills, was also intended to develop their digital literacy and empathy (i.e. being 'socially responsible while strategically using digital media' [Chen, 2018: 50]). For the project, students first watched two documentaries that dealt with different issues online (e.g. cyber-bullying). Next, students wrote scripts, had their scripts peer reviewed and then recorded three-minute reflection videos. Although Chen noted that students' videos were uploaded to a classroom Facebook page, the specific software and tools used for creating the videos were not mentioned.

Once students had completed their videos, Chen (2018) collected them and then distributed a questionnaire. The questionnaire gauged learners' perceptions of the task, and it consisted of both open-ended and closed items, in which students rated the closed items on a 5-point Likert scale (5 = strongly agree, 1 = strongly disagree). Following an analysis of the data, Chen reported that the students generally had very positive perceptions of the digital video project, with a mean (M) rating of 4.4 (SD = 0.8). Students also felt that the digital video project was an effective activity that enabled them to learn about digital empathy (M = 4.6, SD = 0.7). In terms of students' comments on the open-ended questionnaire items, students again appeared to have positive perceptions. For instance, the learners reported enjoying the multi-stage nature of the project, especially when it came to areas such as developing their video production skills, engaging in active listening and receiving feedback from their peers. Importantly, the students also provided comments for improving the project in future iterations, such as integrating short readings about the topics.

The next study is Kim and Belcher (2020). This study was briefly discussed in Chapter 4 as one of the authors' research questions focused on investigating the topic of *outcomes and evidence of learning*. However, Kim and Belcher's study is also relevant to this chapter, as they had a second research question that focused on the topic of students' perceptions. As a reminder, Kim and Belcher were motivated by multiliteracies and were interested in investigating the extent to which DMC tasks compared to traditional monomodal argumentative essays. Their study was set in the context of a university-level L2 English writing course in South Korea, and 18 learners took part in the study. These students were given one month to complete both a traditional essay and a DMC project as homework. The prompt asked the students to apply for a job, and as part of their applications, they needed to (1) compose a traditional argumentative essay on a topic of their choice and (2) create a DMC project on the same topic. The DMC task appeared to be left open to students, as further details were not provided. However, for the planning stage of the DMC project, students engaged in storyboarding, and they also wrote a script for oral narration purposes.

In addition to collecting students' argumentative essays and DMC projects, Kim and Belcher (2020) collected project reflection journals and a post-study survey that assessed students' perspectives of the two tasks. The survey consisted of six open-ended questions that asked about areas such as students' enjoyment of the two tasks, and which task they found to be more effective. Following a thematic analysis of students' survey comments, Kim and Belcher reported that 72% of the students stated that they enjoyed the DMC task more than the traditional essay. Interestingly, there was an even split (50-50) when it came to students stating which task they found to be more helpful for learning English. Most students (67%) perceived the traditional essay as promoting more attention to linguistic form, but 100% of the students stated that they found the DMC task to be more effective for communicating with and attracting an audience.

The final study to be showcased here on the theme of students' perspectives is Kohnke *et al.* (2021). Like Castañeda (2013) and Chen (2018), Kohnke *et al.* (2021) investigated students' perceptions of a specific DMC task, which in their study was the use of infographics. Infographics are a common digital multimodal genre, which aim to 'break down complex information by integrating data via diagrams and text in a graphic format' (Kohnke *et al.*, 2021: 4). The study took place at a university in Hong Kong with 12 undergraduates who were enrolled in an English for Specific Purposes course. For the course, the researchers investigated the use of infographics for language assessment purposes, and they were interested in understanding students' perspectives of its utility in this capacity. For the assignment, students were required to reflect on their learning processes and major projects they had completed for their academic disciplines. Students were required to integrate other non-linguistic modes (e.g. images and graphs) with approximately 300 words of text, and they were asked to guide their audience through the topic in a 'reader-friendly way' (Kohnke *et al.*, 2021: 5). The software and digital tools used for creating the infographics were not specified.

On completion of the assignment, Kohnke *et al.* (2021) conducted semi-structured interviews with each of the 12 participants. They asked students questions about their thoughts on the use of infographics as a form of assessment, how authentic students found the task to be (i.e. if they might encounter or use infographics in their future careers) and more. An analysis of the data found multiple recurring themes that emerged from students' responses. Notably, three students stated that they felt it was a meaningful, real-world task, with one student remarking that in the future, 'this is actually how I'll tell the client my design ideas' (Kohnke *et al.*, 2021: 7). Because it was directly relevant to their future workplaces, five students also stated that the task improved their self-confidence in their ability to succeed. Finally, in terms of using infographics for English language assessment purposes, some students found it suitable, but one learner remarked that he would have preferred to write more monomodal texts, stating: 'I think we are not really helping our English skills. If we write more, I can improve' (Kohnke *et al.*, 2021: 9).

## Studies comparing teachers' and students' perceptions

The third and final theme presented here pertains to those studies that have directly compared teachers' and students' perceptions of DMC. As referenced earlier in this chapter, these types of studies are relatively rare. However, comparisons of both groups' beliefs about the use of DMC in the classroom are important, especially since research in other domains of applied linguistics has shown that teachers may have a tendency to have various misconceptions about phenomena pertaining to their learners (e.g. Ahmadian *et al.*, 2017; Kessler *et al.*, 2020b; Murphy, 2003).

One of the few studies in this domain is Thang *et al.* (2014), in which the researchers investigated teachers' and students' perceptions of a digital storytelling task, as it was integrated into multiple sections of an English for Academic Purposes (EAP) course. The study took place at a university in Malaysia, with 201 students and five teachers. In the EAP course, groups of four or five students were assigned a digital storytelling task as a final course project. The project consisted of four stages: an introduction (by the teacher to the task), a description of the digital story (with students submitting a short description of their story via a blog), digital story experiences (with students individually reflecting on their own experiences with the project) and a digital story presentation (with group presentations of the stories to the entire class). The topic for students' digital stories appeared to be open-ended, as it was not clearly specified in the article. Students were provided with training on how to use Photo Story 3 for completing their DMC projects.

To gauge the teachers' perceptions, all five teachers were interviewed at the end of the semester. To understand the students' perceptions, the researchers designed a questionnaire with 31 items that assessed students' beliefs about different aspects of the DMC task, such as its ability to foster autonomous learning and to promote L2 skills. Students then rated these 31 items on a 4-point Likert scale (4 = strongly agree, 1 = strongly disagree). In their results, Thang *et al.* (2014) indicated that the students generally had favorable impressions of the digital storytelling project. Students reported enjoying the collaborative nature of the project, which they felt had the capacity to promote EAP skills development. The teachers also agreed that the collaborative design of the project was effective for their students, and that the multi-stage nature of the DMC task facilitated learners' development of L2 oral and writing skills. Although most teachers had positive perceptions, one teacher disagreed. Specifically, this teacher stated that he felt it was not appropriate for lower-proficiency students and that the task was challenging to implement.

Jiang (2017) is the final study discussed here that investigated both teachers' and students' perceptions of DMC. Like Thang *et al.* (2014), Jiang was interested in understanding the application of DMC in a university EFL context. Jiang's study was motivated in part by social semiotics (e.g. Kress, 2003, 2010), and his research took place in China, where a year-long DMC program was instituted. As part of the intermediate-level L2 English courses at the university, teachers introduced their students to different digital tools (not specified), and students were required to produce five different digital videos. The videos, each between two and eight minutes long, corresponded to five different curricular units, and students were given between four and six weeks to complete each assignment. As is typical with digital video projects, students participated in different tasks, such as engaging in scriptwriting, collecting and creating multimodal resources, and producing and editing sound recordings.

In terms of data, Jiang (2017) recruited 5 teachers and 22 students at the end of the year, who engaged in semi-structured interviews about their experiences. Both teachers and students also wrote reflections about their experiences, in which they were asked to comment on the affordances of DMC. Following data analysis, Jiang reported three themes that emerged from participants' interviews and reflections: *technological affordances*, *educational affordances* and *social affordances*. For technological affordances, teachers and students felt that the digital recorded nature of the projects enabled learners to take more ownership of their work and to invest more time in it. For educational affordances, all five teachers and 21 students agreed that it enabled students to use English for more authentic and communicative purposes when compared to more traditional forms of L2 instruction. Lastly, in terms of social affordances, similar to Thang *et al.* (2014), Jiang (2017) reported that the teachers and students enjoyed the social and collaborative atmosphere that the digital videos promoted, since many students routinely helped each other with technical aspects of making their videos and also shared their final videos with each other.

## Implications for Researchers

Based on the studies reviewed in this chapter, the implications for researchers who may be interested in examining teachers' and/or students' perceptions of DMC in the future are discussed. Beginning with the studies that investigated teachers' perceptions only, readers of this chapter may have noticed that of the studies outlined here, most researchers have tended to focus on the beliefs of novice or pre-service teachers in-training (e.g. Li, 2020; Normann, 2022; Tan & Matsuda, 2020). That is to say, of the focal participants for the aforementioned teacher perception studies, most participants were likely selected on the basis of convenience sampling, with the teacher-participants being members of the researchers' local academic department, graduate program or classroom. This, in itself, is not an issue. However, given the fact that many studies have now thoroughly examined novice and pre-service teachers' perceptions, researchers must now turn their attention to more practiced and experienced teachers.

Scholarship in related areas involving teacher identity and classroom pedagogy has consistently shown that it is critical to investigate both novice and experienced teachers' perspectives, especially since there may be stark differences in teachers' beliefs and practices that depend on experience, instructional context and more (e.g. Ajayi, 2011; Kessler, 2021a; Mok, 1994). This is also vital in the area of CALL. Similarly, a teacher's age, educational training, experience level and other factors may all play prominent roles in influencing one's subsequent perceptions and practices (e.g. Lee *et al.*, 2011; Li *et al.*, 2019). As such, studies are now needed that explore experienced teachers' perceptions of DMC when used in the classroom. For instance, for experienced teachers who adopt more traditional methods and monomodal writing activities in their courses, what are their thoughts and perceptions when asked to implement DMC for teaching L2 writing? What are the experiences of these teachers when they actually do adopt DMC for the first time? That is, what successes and challenges do they experience during the process? Would these teachers continue using DMC in the future (and why or why not)? Relatedly, future studies are also needed that attempt to facilitate direct comparisons between experienced and novice teachers who are working in the same or similar instructional contexts. For instance, to what extent do teachers of different ages and experience levels perceive DMC similarly or differently in the same context? What other factors may contribute to their perceptions? Currently, these are questions that remain unanswered.

In this chapter, Ryu and Boggs (2016) was one of the only studies to explore (relatively) more experienced teachers' perceptions. However, as noted earlier, in Ryu and Boggs' research design, they stated that they purposefully sampled for teachers who already adopted DMC as a part of their instructional practices. While it was interesting to learn more about how and why these teachers adopted DMC in their test-heavy context of South Korea, Ryu and Boggs' sampling also points to a broader, more general issue in many CALL studies. Specifically, this issue is a tendency for researchers to focus *only* on the affordances of the target technology, tool or software. Apart from Ryu and Boggs' study, Jiang (2017) is another illustration of this issue. For instance, in Jiang's study, it appears that the researcher only asked his focal teachers and students about DMC's affordances. In the study, both of the research questions specifically mentioned the word 'affordances' (Jiang, 2017: 415). As further evidence, when describing what the focal teachers and students were required to discuss in their interviews and written reflections, Jiang (2017: 415) stated that the participants 'recorded their comments on the *possibilities* created by DMC for EFL learning' (*italics* added for emphasis). That is, it seems that the participants were directed to focus only on the possibilities and affordances of DMC (in a positive sense), and thus, they may have avoided discussing any negative perceptions they had about the activities. Of course, from the perspective of a researcher, it is important to understand the affordances of various CALL activities and tools. However, it can be argued that it is equally important to understand the potential drawbacks or negative impacts of a tool's use. Thus, for future studies of teachers' (and students') perspectives, researchers should strongly consider investigating all of their participants' beliefs, and not only those beliefs that may shine a positive light on DMC.

In moving to research that investigated students' perceptions, perhaps one of the most interesting studies covered in this chapter is Kim and Belcher (2020). In particular, Kim and Belcher's study is unique because it is one of the few studies to pose research questions that address both students' perceptions *and* actual aspects of those L2 learners' writing performance. Thus, their study is noteworthy in that it has the capacity to compare DMC's efficacy as judged by subjective measures (i.e. students' opinions) and objective linguistic measures (i.e. measures of syntactic complexity and accuracy). As discussed in Chapter 4, following an analysis of students' traditional essays and DMCs, Kim and Belcher reported that the traditional essay was more syntactically complex with a small to medium effect size. However, there were no significant differences between the two compositions in terms of accuracy. Similarly, the students' perceptions were somewhat mixed in reflecting these results, as many students (67%) perceived the traditional essay as promoting more attention to language form.

Although Kim and Belcher's (2020) findings are somewhat difficult to interpret, in general, this speaks to the need for more studies of a similar nature. For instance, future studies might investigate related topics, such as students' perceptions of monomodal writing tasks versus DMC tasks. When doing so, researchers might examine the extent to which learners perceive one task as being more effective than (or equally effective as) the other in terms of writing quality, and also, which task learners believe promotes more attention to complexity, accuracy and fluency. In the same vein, students' perceptions might also be investigated when engaging in two different DMC tasks. For instance, do students perceive one DMC task (e.g. digital storytelling versus infographics) as more conducive for SLA purposes? If so, why? To what extent do students' perspectives of these tasks align with objective linguistic measures or other learning outcomes? Finally, to what extent do students' beliefs align with their teachers' beliefs regarding such tasks?

**Implications for Teachers**

This final section now shifts from a discussion of implications for researchers to implications for teachers. In particular, because of the highly pedagogical nature and focus of the studies reviewed in this chapter, there are a number of meaningful ramifications for classroom practitioners. The first two implications pertain to the different issues involved in teachers setting up various DMC tasks. Firstly, in Li's (2020) study of pre-service teachers, despite the participants' overwhelming positivity in response to the two DMC projects that Li instituted in her graduate courses, the researcher also noted that some of her participants reported experiencing challenges when it came to engaging in the DMC tasks. Namely, although the task type for the projects was clearly specified for the students, the topic of the students' projects was left relatively open-ended for the learners to select on their own. This open-endedness of the prompt caused some students to struggle with topic selection, remarking that they found it to be somewhat 'daunting' (Li, 2020: 8) since they could select anything that was covered during the span of the semester-long course. In addition to difficulties with topic selection, other students remarked that they struggled due to their unfamiliarity with the technology platforms since no training was provided in class.

Thus, when implementing DMC in the future, the issues of topic selection and technological literacy are two things that teachers need to be conscious of in their practice. That is, since it is likely that learners may struggle with topic selection and gaining familiarity with the software needed to complete the DMC task, it may be best to anticipate these issues and attempt to remove these obstacles when setting up the task. In terms of topic selection, this can be addressed by giving students a list of sample topics to choose from when completing their DMCs, in addition to providing learners with an open-ended 'student's choice' option for a topic. In terms of technology issues, this could be addressed by giving students the relevant training and time they need to gain familiarity with the software. Since the software and digital tools may already be familiar to some of the students in the classroom, teachers should consider briefly polling their students before the task to see who has experience with them. If some students do have experience (which is often the case), these students can serve as go-to guides for their peers and help them problem solve any technology-related issues that may arise.

Related to setting up the DMC task, the second issue again pertains to giving students the appropriate resources that they need prior to engaging in the task. This implication arises from Normann (2022), in which, after drafting their digital stories, some participants stated that they found it challenging to find pictures on the internet, so they ended up drawing their own illustrations because they found this to be faster. Although a quick Google search is often an easy way to find images, videos and other modal resources, depending on the nature of the project itself, it may also be necessary to give students a list of sample resources and tips to help aid their online searches. For instance, there are a number of free, open-access resources that students can use for creating their DMC projects. These resources include online repositories such as Creative Commons (creativecommons.org), Mazwai (mazwai.com) and Pexels (pexels.com), which allow students to download and use copyright-free content for non-commercial purposes. These resources are described in further detail in Chapter 7, which covers commonly used DMC tasks, activities and resources. However, prior to implementing a DMC task in the classroom, it can be extremely beneficial for teachers to share these existing resources with their students. It can also be helpful for teachers to clearly articulate ahead of time if a project is likely to be primarily student driven in terms of the production of modal resources (e.g. storyboards with linguistic text and illustrations), or if many of the resources will need to come from existing media (e.g. digital video projects with stock footage, videos and music). Based on what the focal DMC project requires, teachers should give students the appropriate means for finding and creating their projects at the pre-task phase.

Another pedagogical implication pertains to using DMC as a multistage project for reflective learning purposes. For instance, in Castañeda's (2013) article, during the process of engaging in a digital storytelling task, multiple students noted that they enjoyed the opportunity to review and edit their own work. They stated that they particularly liked how the reflective nature of the task enabled them to catch their own mistakes and to increase their self-awareness of their personal issues with the target language. Thus, Castañeda's students were able to consciously notice gaps in their interlanguage (see Schmidt, 1990), and they were able to revise and re-record parts of their videos upon noticing their mistakes.

Because students have reported enjoying such reflective tasks in both Castañeda (2013) and other studies, teachers may wish to consider experimenting with other pedagogical activities that have the capacity to promote noticing and self-reflection. As an example, multiple studies within the domain of CALL have shown the potential of transcription activities for promoting conscious noticing (e.g. Cowie, 2018; Kessler et al., 2020a; Loewen et al., 2022). Although transcription was not specifically discussed by any of the studies in this chapter, teachers could integrate transcription activities with DMC tasks (and do so with relative ease). For example, when assigning something like a digital video project, teachers might consider implementing a stage in which learners are required to select a short, recorded passage of their own speech or that of their peers, and then transcribe that speech. Students might then be encouraged to look for the target grammar or vocabulary points covered in class and to engage in self or peer review of the transcription. This would be an easy and effective way to facilitate self-reflection and noticing.

The final pedagogical recommendation provided here once again has to do with how DMC tasks are configured by the teacher. Of the studies in this chapter that have investigated students' perceptions of DMC tasks, multiple studies such as Jiang (2017) and Thang et al. (2014) have expressed a clear, underlying theme: that students appear to enjoy DMC projects when they are collaborative in nature. This particularly seems to be the case in EFL and other foreign language contexts, where the students may be limited in the number of opportunities that they have to engage in meaningful, authentic tasks with the target language. Interestingly, in those studies of students' perceptions where learners tended to work more independently, one of the comments that students made was that they wished that more collaboration was integrated into the task. For example, in Castañeda (2013), after completing their project, most students stated that they enjoyed the task, but some remarked that they felt it could be improved by allowing learners to interact and talk more with each other.

Since learners have consistently reported enjoying DMC when it is adopted as a collaborative endeavor, teachers should strongly consider integrating a collaborative activity or component when adopting DMC. This, of course, does not mean that the entire DMC project must be collaborative. However, because many DMC tasks require learners to complete multiple stages (e.g. digital video projects, digital storytelling), when using such tasks, it is relatively easy to find ways to have students work with a partner or in small groups during different phases of the project. With other DMC tasks that do not consist of numerous stages (e.g. storyboards, digital posters), teachers may need to be more creative. One option is to make the task completely collaborative with learners working with a peer(s) when completing it. Another option is to institute different collaborative components such as a shared pre-task planning stage (e.g. brainstorming), having peers assist each other with searching for/finding visuals online, having students engage in peer review or, perhaps, making the final presentation of students' DMC projects collaborative in nature, with peers commenting on and reviewing others' final works. Thus, regardless of the DMC task, teachers may wish to consider making all or parts of the task interactive and collaborative in nature.

# 6 Individual Differences

**Introduction**

The previous research-oriented chapters have highlighted studies where scholars have examined topics such as students' *writing processes* (Chapter 3), *outcomes and evidence of learning* (Chapter 4) and *teachers' and students' perceptions* (Chapter 5). This final research-focused chapter now turns to a discussion of digital multimodal composing's (DMC) influence on *individual differences* (IDs). The topic of IDs has received substantial attention in other scientific fields of inquiry (e.g. psychology) for some time, yet in the fields of applied linguistics and second language acquisition (SLA), IDs have only recently started to gain traction over the past two decades (e.g. Ellis, 2004, 2022; Li *et al.*, 2022a; Ortega, 2009). As defined by Li *et al.* (2022b: 3), IDs refer to 'learner traits and characteristics that may have an impact on learning processes, behaviors, and outcomes'. There are numerous IDs that may come into play during the second language (L2) learning process, and these IDs can be broadly classified into different types or categories. These include IDs that are *cognitive* in nature (e.g. a learner's aptitude, working memory and metacognition), *conative* (e.g. motivation and willingness to communicate), *affective* (e.g. anxiety and enjoyment) and *demographic/sociocultural* (e.g. age and identity). Broadly speaking, when it comes to L2 learning outcomes, understanding IDs has been recognized as an important consideration because a number of studies within the SLA literature have demonstrated that learner-internal factors such as anxiety, enjoyment, motivation and working memory can often explain or account for a sizable percentage of learners' overall success with a target language (e.g. Alrabai, 2022; Dewaele *et al.*, 2017; Mitchell *et al.*, 2015).

Arguably, IDs have received the most attention when investigated in conjunction with other areas of SLA, such as L2 learners' performance on measures pertaining to grammatical competence and pronunciation. That being said, IDs have also been demonstrated to play an influential role in learning and the development of L2 writing skills. For instance, L2 writing scholarship investigating IDs has shown that various learner characteristics have the capacity to influence students' writing behaviors (e.g. their engagement with corrective feedback and their feedback-seeking behaviors), and to impact learners' ultimate attainment of written linguistic forms (e.g. Han, 2017; Kessler, 2023b; Tahmouresi & Papi, 2021; Waller & Papi, 2017). Because of this, Papi *et al.* (2022) have argued that understanding the role of IDs in L2 writing is essential, especially since learning to master L2 writing skills is a cognitively complex and challenging endeavor. This sentiment expressed by Papi *et al.* is one that has also been shared by many computer-assisted language learning (CALL) scholars, and particularly by those researchers who are interested in multimodal writing and DMC. Specifically, there is a growing recognition that digital technologies and the availability of different (non-linguistic) modal resources may have the capacity to foster the development of a small number of IDs.

As such, this chapter focuses on the increasingly important topic of IDs within the domain of L2 writing, and specifically, this chapter examines those studies that have investigated the influence of DMC tasks on IDs. As mentioned earlier, numerous IDs have been explored across the broader fields of applied linguistics and SLA (see Li *et al.*'s [2022a] handbook for a comprehensive review). However, when it comes to DMC, researchers have typically focused on a select number of targets. This chapter segments research into three major ID categories or themes. These themes consist of studies that explore DMC's impact on L2 learners' (1) *identity*, (2) *motivation* and (3) *metacognition*. In keeping with the previous research-focused chapters, for each of these themes, multiple studies are presented that sit at the intersection of DMC and ID research, with each study described in depth as a means of highlighting key information. This includes illustrating features of the studies' designs, the focal DMC task/activity used, the student populations involved and various other aspects of the studies' methods and findings. For each theme, studies are once again presented chronologically by date of publication, from oldest to newest.

## Research: Key Findings

### Identity

When it comes to DMC research involving IDs, DMC's influence on aspects of learners' *identities* has received considerable attention. Identity itself has been a topic of great interest to researchers in numerous fields including both education and applied linguistics (e.g. Block, 2007; De Costa & Norton, 2016; Yuan, 2019). Because of this, it has sometimes been conceptualized and defined differently. Notably, within the applied linguistics literature, Norton (2013: 45) has described the construct of identity as 'how a person understands his or her relationship to the world, [and] how that relationship is structured across time and space'.

Identity is seen as an influential construct within applied linguistics and SLA for a number of reasons. For example, experienced language teachers may adopt different identities for various social or functional purposes when in the classroom, while novice or pre-service teachers in training may struggle with developing their identities and need careful support and scaffolding throughout the process of becoming a teacher (e.g. Farrell, 2011; Karimi & Mofidi, 2019; Martel, 2019). For L2 writers, too, identity is instrumental. This is because how writers choose to represent or portray themselves can be extremely impactful when composing texts for L2 testing purposes or when applying for competitive grant opportunities; likewise, discovering one's identity as an L2 writer may be both challenging and a site of struggle (e.g. Kessler, 2022b; Li & Deng, 2019; Supasiraprapa & De Costa, 2017).

In terms of DMC research on the topic of identity, one of the earliest studies to explore this area is Pyo (2016). In her qualitative case study, Pyo examined how one L2 English learner cultivated his literate identity when engaging in multimodal composing. The focal student, John (a pseudonym), was an L1 Korean speaker in an 8th-grade English class in the Midwestern United States. Pyo (2016: 421) was interested in John's case because, as she noted, while at school, John 'struggled to focus on his studies and rarely invested himself in the assigned coursework'. Yet, when at home, John was an active reader and writer, primarily of digital materials. As such, Pyo was motivated by multiliteracies (New London Group, 1996), and she particularly felt that a multimodal assignment might appeal to John by enabling him to represent himself in ways that more traditional, monomodal assignments might not. Therefore, Pyo implemented a project in her 8th-grade class in which students first read an assigned book and then took turns leading discussions following each chapter. After completing the book, students were required to choose one of four provided topics that had previously been discussed (e.g. stereotypes, making friends). Students created a multimodal project that was relatively open-ended (e.g. digital video, digital storytelling) to describe the selected theme from the book. Most students, including John, opted for a digital storytelling task via Microsoft PowerPoint, and students were required to share their narratives orally in class.

To understand John's case, Pyo (2016) collected data that included his PowerPoint slideshow presentation and in-class observations (as his teacher), and she also conducted interviews with the student at his home. Following data analysis, Pyo (2016: 425) remarked that John was particularly engaged in the DMC project, with John himself noting that when working on it, 'time just flew by… This is different from what I usually do at school'. Through analyzing the slides of his PowerPoint, the researcher noted how John orchestrated various modes and constructed his identity as an author, something he seemed reluctant to do when engaging in other monomodal reading and writing tasks during her course. Thus, Pyo's (2016: 427) study is noteworthy not only because it shows how the DMC task enabled a young L2 learner to 'compensate for his limitations in English', but also because it appeared to offer him an additional means to develop his voice and identity as a writer.

The next study on identity that is showcased is by Jiang *et al.* (2020). Unlike Pyo's (2016) study, Jiang *et al.*'s research took place in an English as a foreign language (EFL) context in China, in which the authors were interested in investigating the experiences of an ethnic minority student in a mainstream classroom. As the authors noted, ethnic minority students often struggle in English language classrooms for a number of reasons, including a comparative lack of access to linguistic capital and challenges with finding quality English learning resources in their local communities. Therefore, the authors were interested in understanding DMC's influence (particularly the influence of non-linguistic modes) on the literacy practices and identities of an L2 English learner. Jiang *et al.*'s study took place at a coastal university in China. The researchers focused on one ethnic minority student from Tibet named Tashi, who was enrolled in a university-level English class with a majority of ethnic Han Chinese students. As part of a larger DMC programmatic initiative, in the course, the teacher implemented six DMC projects over the span of two academic semesters. In the projects, students created multiple digital videos in response to different topics discussed in class (not specified) – first collaboratively and then individually – in which they combined oral and textual linguistic modes with visuals, soundtracks and more. Students were provided with workshops on how to storyboard, shoot and edit their videos; however, the software and digital tools used for creating the videos were not specified.

In order to understand Tashi's experiences, the researchers conducted a longitudinal case study and collected various forms of data such as classroom observations, semi-structured interviews, written reflections and the student's digital videos. Content analysis was used to analyze the data, and the researchers paid particular attention to shifts in Tashi's identity and how her classroom participation and interactions evolved over time. In their findings, Jiang *et al.* (2020: 965) showcased how Tashi initially felt a sense of 'fear' and 'inferiority' compared to her Han Chinese peers, especially about learning English. This led Tashi to state that 'attending English class is a big phobia to me' (Jiang *et al.*, 2020: 996). However, throughout the process of collaboratively engaging in the digital video projects, Tashi's tone slowly changed, along with her enjoyment and willingness to communicate with her classmates. Afterward, when individually working on a digital video, interview data revealed that Tashi began to 'accept herself as a qualified English speaker through the technological affordance of DMC' (Jiang *et al.*, 2020: 968). The repeated use of DMC projects emboldened her to speak not only on class topics, but also on her Tibetan background and knowledge of Tibetan culture. Thus, Tashi grew increasingly confident and positive about her ethnic identity. As these data show, Jiang *et al.*'s study is particularly well executed in its investigation of DMC and identity. For one, it shows how the use of collaborative and individual DMC projects may empower minority students to embrace their ethnic identities. Also, it touches upon other important IDs, including how willingness to communicate may be affected by using DMC.

The third study presented on the topic of identity is Liaw and Accurso (2021), which was motivated by multiliteracies. In the study, the researchers analyzed the affordances of multimodal composing pedagogy for K-12 students' literacy building and identity development. Their study took place in a 5th-grade Chinese–English dual immersion classroom in the United States. Similar to Jiang *et al.* (2020), Liaw and Accurso's research was a year-long ethnographic case study, which focused on one learner. The focal student was a 5th-grader named Mei-mei. The researchers stated that they selected Mei-mei because, despite her strong literacy skills and motivation to learn, 'her L2 literacy development was progressing more slowly than she wanted' (Liaw & Accurso, 2021: 95). As part of the course, Mei-mei and the other students were engaging with the topic of state history (in this particular case, the state of Massachusetts). After learning about the state's history, as a culminating project, the classroom teacher asked the students to compose a digital video project, in which students were required to present multiple perspectives on one aspect of the state's history. When creating their digital videos, students produced them on iPads using the app Explain Everything, and they combined media, images, text and voice recordings.

In terms of data, Liaw and Accurso (2021) engaged in repeated classroom observations, took field notes and collected audio and video recordings of class sessions along with the focal student's work. A grounded theory approach was used to analyze themes that emerged from the data (see Charmaz, 2014), along with multimodal discourse analysis (see D'Angelo & Marino, 2024, for more). Following their analyses, Liaw and Accurso (2021: 100, italics in original) noted that the inclusion of the digital video project enabled the focal participant to become 'a critical thinker, a designer of meanings, an oral narrator, *and* an L2 writer'. Through her digital video, Mei-mei positioned herself as a knowledgeable person about the state's history, and she also excelled when using both English and Chinese. Importantly, interview excerpts from Mei-mei illustrated that as a learner, she understood that the multimodal composition required her to think in different ways, and she subsequently responded to this challenge in a positive manner by constructing 'a biliterate identity' as a competent user of the two target languages (Liaw & Accurso, 2021: 101). Thus, the DMC process itself served as a boon to the student's literacy and identity development.

The final DMC-focused study involving identity is by Dávila and Susberry (2021). In their qualitative case study, the researchers explored how adolescent L2 English learners engaged in the production of multimodal texts, and how those projects influenced aspects of their transnational civic identities. The study took place in the context of two public high school English as a second language (ESL) classrooms in the United States, which had a curricular focus on social studies and civics. Data were collected from seven students between the ages of 14 and 18, all of whom were multilingual speakers of French and additional languages (e.g. Lingala). The students completed multiple collaborative writing assignments such as a multimodal poster, and they also engaged in producing, recording and performing a screenplay, which focused on the topic of peoples' immigration experiences. For the projects, students worked in groups of three or four for two weeks. The tools used for creating and recording the screenplays were not specified.

To investigate aspects of the learners' identities, Dávila and Susberry (2021) collected data such as students' written work (posters, screenplays), screen recordings of students' classroom interactions and classroom observations and field notes. In total, 23 writing samples were collected, but Dávila and Susberry (2021: 61) noted that only three were presented in their study because 'they showcase[d] how the focal students singularly and collectively navigate[d] languages, experiences, and identities as they negotiate[d] means of expressing themselves through text and images'. Dávila and Susberry's (2021: 66) findings illustrate how the collaborative multimodal composition process fostered expressions of 'transnational civic identities (of belonging both here and there)'. The screenplay assignment afforded learners the opportunity to understand the personal stories of their peers, in addition to engaging with notions of belonging and exclusion. In terms of the poster, students produced posters as displays for a school event, which showcased the languages and cultures of the learners in the school. Students integrated linguistic text describing their French backgrounds (e.g. words such as *travail* [work/labor]), their English backgrounds and numerous images, showcasing their identities to the wider audience of the school. Dávila and Susberry closed their piece by noting the pedagogical utility of such assignments, which they state can be used to positively develop the identities of transnational students who may face marginalization in society.

## Motivation

The second ID discussed in this chapter is *motivation*. Although the topic of identity has received much attention during the past two decades in the fields of applied linguistics and SLA, perhaps no topic has been researched more extensively than that of motivation (e.g. Dörnyei, 1994,

2009; Gardner & MacIntyre, 1991; Gardner & Smythe, 1975; Kormos, 2012; Yu et al., 2020). This is because, as Papi and Hiver (2022: 113) have noted, 'second language (L2) learning is fundamentally a motivational pursuit'; importantly, as they go on to state, a learner's motivation – i.e. the phenomenon that 'explains the direction, vigor, and persistence of actions', including 'why we do or do not take a certain course of actions versus others' – may be influenced by a number of internal and external factors. Without question, numerous studies have demonstrated the importance of motivation in learning an additional language. By extension, understanding DMC's impact on aspects of L2 learners' motivation has also been a topic of much interest.

Yang and Wu (2012) is the first study showcased in this section, in which the researchers investigated the impact of digital storytelling tasks on the motivation, academic achievement and critical thinking skills of L2 English learners. Among the studies discussed in this chapter, Yang and Wu's study is notable because the researchers adopted a quasi-experimental design. Also somewhat unique is that rather than discussing the potential affordances of multimodality, Yang and Wu were primarily motivated by sociocultural theory (Vygotsky, 1978) and understanding the extent to which students' collaborations using various digital tools impacted their motivation and learning. The study took place at a high school in Taiwan, in which the researchers recruited 110 students from two 10th-grade English classes. One class ($n = 56$) served as the control group and was taught using a traditional lecture-style approach with monomodal writing assignments. The other class ($n = 54$) served as the experimental group. Over 22 weeks, the experimental group completed multiple digital storytelling tasks in which they collaboratively created digital stories on various topics (e.g. telling the stories of the eight planets, traditional Chinese festivals). When creating their digital stories, students were given the choice of multiple options, including Microsoft Photo Story 3 and Microsoft Movie Maker.

To investigate the influence of repeated digital storytelling tasks on the outcome variables, Yang and Wu (2012) adopted a pretest-posttest design, with the pretest administered in Week 1 and the posttest administered in Week 22. For assessing learners' motivation, the authors used a questionnaire developed by Wu and Cherng (1992), in which students rated 11 items using a 6-point (true-of-me) Likert scale. Critical thinking was also assessed using an existing test (see Yeh, 2003), but the English achievement test was developed by the researchers to correspond to class content. Both analysis of covariances (ANCOVA) and multivariate analysis of covariances (MANCOVA) were used to assess the statistical differences between the two groups on the three tests, including their various constructs. The results showed that the DMC tasks motivated the experimental group significantly more than traditional instructional methods. This was especially the case in terms of the DMC group's motivation toward *task value* (i.e. 'students' judgments on the interest, usefulness, and importance' of the task) (Wu & Cherng, 1992: 342). In terms of critical thinking, the experimental group also outgained the control group with a large effect size. This finding also held true for academic achievement, with the DMC group performing significantly better than the control group with a large effect size, particularly in the areas of listening and reading skills. Thus, Yang and Wu's (2012) study is noteworthy for its large participant pool, use of quantitative methods and its longitudinal design.

The next study highlighted is Henry (2019). This study took place in the context of a seventh-grade classroom in Sweden, in which 13-year-old learners of L2 English engaged in a blogging project. Henry (2019: 377) noted that in the focal context, Swedish students typically have 'extensive encounters with English outside the classroom', so one challenge that teachers face is how 'to create learning opportunities that connect with these out-of-school experiences'. Therefore, Henry was interested in investigating the influence of a blogging task on students' motivation, and particularly, the extent to which this authentic task might spur students' motivation over time. To do so, Henry conducted an ethnographic multiple case study of a five-week long blogging project. For the project, students created a blog about an imaginary trip to an English-speaking country of their choice. Students were required to make daily posts, to use the internet to search for factual information about the target country, and they were also given sample topics to consider discussing (e.g. climate, religion, time differences and food). They were also provided with a list of possible blogging platforms such as Nouw, Blogg.se and Devote.se.

In terms of data, Henry (2019) conducted fieldwork, which included observing nine classroom lessons, keeping detailed field notes, collecting students' online blog posts and conducting a focus group interview with four students. Grounded theory was used to analyze the data and uncover emergent themes. In his findings, Henry drew on various field notes and excerpts from focus group interviews with students, noting that many students found the blogging task to be motivational because it merged both their leisure-time practices and schoolwork. Students were particularly motivated by the idea that a real-life audience might be viewing their blogs, which encouraged attention to detail and an investment in making the blogs both accurate and visually appealing. Henry also compared and contrasted different groups of students who worked together, highlighting that while some all-female groups appeared to maintain a consistently high level of motivation, it fluctuated in some of the all-male or mixed-gender groups. Thus, Henry noted that overall, the blogging task appeared to be a motivator that was well liked by the students. However, additional IDs (e.g. gender) and social factors (e.g.

group dynamics) may also be important to investigate when examining DMC's impact on motivation.

The third and final study highlighted for the ID of motivation is Hava (2021), in which the researcher examined the extent to which EFL learners' motivation and satisfaction were influenced by the adoption of a digital storytelling task. Hava (2021: 959) herself was motivated to explore this topic due to what she cited as 'unsuccessful' English language polices, practices and standards in Turkey 'for many years' which negatively impacted students' L2 learning and motivation. Hava recruited 60 pre-service English teachers (between 18 and 21 years old), who were enrolled in two compulsory undergraduate English language classes. Information regarding students' proficiency level(s) is somewhat unclear, although it was stated that students were taking the course because they had not passed the university's English proficiency exam. No students had experience with digital storytelling prior to the study. In terms of the task, over nine weeks, students were required to create three digital stories on assigned topics (i.e. countries, nature and sports). Students received a workshop discussing how to create digital stories, and they were also introduced to platforms such as Openshot, Windows Movie Maker, WeVideo and VivaVideo.

To investigate the impact of the digital storytelling tasks on L2 English learners' motivation and satisfaction, Hava (2021) adopted a pretest-posttest design with one group (i.e. all 60 students). A questionnaire was used to investigate changes in students' motivation over time, and their general satisfaction with the DMC task at the end of the study. The questionnaire for assessing motivation was adopted from a previous study by Mehdiyev *et al.* (2017). This questionnaire consisted of 16 items which students rated using a 5-point Likert scale (totally agree to absolutely disagree), and it assessed three motivational constructs: attitude, self-confidence and personal use. Hava developed the satisfaction questionnaire, and it was only administered at the posttest phase. It included 15 items that were also rated using a 5-point Likert scale, along with open-ended items asking students about their general opinions of the task. Following the use of paired samples *t*-tests to assess differences from pretest to posttest, Hava reported that her students' motivation increased significantly, especially regarding the motivational constructs of self-confidence and personal use. Students also generally appeared to have positive perceptions of the digital storytelling task and its capacity to promote L2 learning and motivation. Finally, some students' qualitative responses pointed to other IDs apart from motivation, such as anxiety (e.g. 'From now on… English is not as difficult as I fear') (Hava, 2021: 969). Thus, Hava's study suggests that DMC tasks such as digital storytelling may have the capacity to improve students' motivation in EFL settings, along with other possible benefits such as reducing anxiety.

## Metacognition

The final ID discussed in this chapter is *metacognition*. Metacognition refers to an individual's awareness of their own thinking, along with an individual's ability to exert control over their thoughts (Flavell, 1979; Schraw & Dennison, 1994). As this definition suggests, metacognition can be divided into two constructs: *metacognitive knowledge* and *metacognitive regulation*. Metacognitive *knowledge* refers to individuals' general awareness of their own thinking, while metacognitive *regulation* refers to people's capacity to control and direct their awareness when completing a task (Brown, 1978; Flavell, 1979; Pintrich, 2004; Schraw, 1998). Broadly speaking, this conscious or explicit awareness of one's own thought processes (and how to control them) has been shown to be a strong predictor of task performance and learning success (Donker *et al.*, 2014). Because of this, in research involving SLA, scholars have been interested in understanding learners' metacognition, and also investigating how different teaching methods and activities may lead to greater metacognitive knowledge and regulation among L2 learners (see Sato [2022] for a review).

Within the domain of L2 writing as well, the topic of metacognition has steadily gained attention over the past decade (e.g. Bui & Kong, 2019; Kessler, 2020b, 2021c; Negretti, 2012, 2017; Negretti & Kuteeva, 2011; Wei, 2020; Yeh, 2015). Primarily, this is because – compared to speaking – the nature of writing itself is slower paced. It thus lends itself to explicit reflection on the part of L2 writers (Williams, 2012). To date, there is relatively limited scholarship involving metacognition and DMC. However, a small number of researchers have investigated DMC's influence on aspects of students' metacognition.

The first of two studies to be showcased on the topic of metacognition is Hung (2019). In the study, Hung noted that prior research on multimodal activities such as digital storytelling has typically focused on aspects of L2 learners' beliefs or learning outcomes. Therefore, Hung was interested in investigating the types of metacognitive skills that L2 English learners employed when engaging in a digital storytelling task. Hung's study took place at a university in Taiwan with 88 third-year students who were enrolled in an English language course. As part of the class, students were assigned a five-week digital storytelling project. Students were allowed to select their own topics (e.g. fashion styles), but all students worked collaboratively in groups of four or five. The project involved various stages, including pre-production (e.g. scriptwriting), production, post-production (e.g. editing) and distribution/sharing. The platforms and tools used for creating the digital stories were not discussed in the article.

For understanding L2 learners' metacognitive skills, Hung (2019) adopted a 10-item questionnaire developed by Goss (2014), which assessed the constructs of goal-setting, planning, monitoring and evaluating one's skills. Students also completed reflections after finishing their digital stories in which they discussed their DMC processes and strategies, among other topics. Since Hung (2019) was interested in examining the types of metacognitive skills that learners used, descriptive statistics were adopted to analyze common trends among the students. In the results, the author reported that the digital storytelling task primarily appeared to encourage monitoring, goal-setting and evaluating. Many of the descriptive quantitative data were later reinforced by qualitative data as well. For instance, in terms of evaluating, multiple students commented on how the task promoted 'checking' their stories and 'checking the[ir] progress and language errors' (Hung, 2019: 34). In closing, Hung noted that DMC tasks such as digital storytelling have the capacity to foster L2 learners' metacognition; however, he also noted that future studies might consider adopting more longitudinal designs to obtain a richer description of such phenomena.

The second and final study presented on the ID of metacognition is Negretti and McGrath (2018). In their study, the authors investigated how L2 English writers' genre knowledge could be scaffolded via two different tasks: a descriptive writing task and a multimodal visualization reflection task. The researchers' qualitative case study looked at the experiences of eight students in doctoral-level programs (e.g. chemistry, physics) at a Swedish technical university. All eight students were enrolled in an English course that focused on developing students' academic research and writing skills. In an effort to promote conscious awareness and attention to various features of academic research articles, the researchers explored the use of two metacognitive tasks, which they stated had the potential to enable students to comprehend information 'beyond their immediate grasp' (Negretti & McGrath, 2018: 16). The first task was a pre-course writing activity in which students discussed their existing knowledge (in response to a writing prompt), thereby activating learners' existing background knowledge of the target genre. Then, after learning about the target genre during class sessions, students completed a visualization reflection task. In this multimodal composing task, students were asked to 'verbalize what [you] know and have learned about [the] topic (in this case genre and research writing)' (Negretti & McGrath, 2018: 17). Learners were directed to 'draw, use computer graphics, paint, [and to] use photos or symbols' (Negretti & McGrath, 2018: 29) to visualize their genre knowledge, and afterward, they were required to write a short commentary in which they reflected on their visuals and what they had learned. Multiple students produced digital multimodal visualizations; however, the tools that they used for creating them were not discussed.

In terms of data analysis, Negretti and McGrath (2018) analyzed students' pre-task written descriptions, their visualization reflections and post-course interview data in which students were asked about their experiences. Negretti and McGrath (2018: 28) reported that the two tasks were successful in 'pushing students to integrate... and verbalize various facets of their genre knowledge'. The multimodal visualization reflection task appeared to be a useful vehicle for helping some students distill and conceptualize their knowledge. Therefore, as the authors contend, researchers and teachers should consider adopting similar visualization activities in the future, particularly as a means of tapping into and scaffolding students' metacognition.

## Implications for Researchers

Now that a review of key studies has been presented, this section turns briefly to discussing the implications for researchers who may be interested in investigating the nexus of DMC and IDs in the future. First and foremost, as referenced in the opening of this chapter, when it comes to ID-oriented research involving DMC, the topics of identity and motivation have typically been the two IDs that have received the most attention. Although identity and motivation continue to remain important and worthy topics of investigation in CALL, L2 writing and applied linguistics more broadly, future research is needed that investigates IDs *beyond* identity and motivation. In particular, quantitative, qualitative or mixed methods studies are needed that further investigate the ID of metacognition, since research in this area is still relatively scarce. Additionally, other IDs are in need of exploration, including age, anxiety, willingness to communicate and working memory. Some of the studies discussed in this chapter (e.g. Hava, 2021) collected ancillary data that touched upon some of these important IDs. However, typically, these IDs have not been the primary focus of authors' attention in their studies, with often only one or two quotes from students that address them in passing. Therefore, more studies are needed that directly examine the influence or use of DMC tasks on a myriad of IDs in order to gain a greater understanding of the potential affordances and limitations of different multimodal tasks.

The second implication for researchers discussed here pertains to the use of multiple DMC tasks and their differential effects on IDs. Of the studies reviewed in this chapter, it should be noted that all of them focused on the implementation of one DMC task and that task's subsequent effects on an ID. Clearly, as mentioned in the previous paragraph, there is still much room for innovative scholarship in this area. However, additional research is now needed that directly compares two (or more) DMC tasks and their resulting influence on specific IDs. For instance, Hava's (2021) study of motivation adopted a digital storytelling task to investigate its influence on her focal learners. Henry's (2019) study of motivation investigated the use of blogs on learners' motivation. Thus, one potentially interesting line of inquiry for future researchers might be to directly compare the motivational effects of these two different tasks. That is, do students find one task to be more motivating than the other (and if so, why)? Or, do students find the two tasks to be equally motivating? This same line of inquiry can be extended to IDs beyond motivation as well (e.g. anxiety, willingness to communicate) since the relative effects of different DMC tasks are currently unknown.

As such, future scholars might consider adopting research designs and corresponding methods that will enable them to make comparisons of the influence of different DMC tasks on IDs. There are numerous ways of designing a study of this nature. For example, such a study might adopt a quantitative repeated-measures design (e.g. with one classroom or group of learners), examining the same L2 learners as they engage in two different tasks during a semester. Another option is to conduct a study that adopts a quasi-experimental between-groups design, in which one classroom of students engages in a DMC task such as digital storytelling, while the second classroom engages in another DMC task such as blogging. Finally, such research could potentially be conducted using qualitative methods, in which a researcher adopts a case study design to investigate the experiences of a small number of L2 learners who engage in multiple DMC tasks over the span of an academic semester. Currently, because there is a general lack of literature in this area, any future studies that can speak to the comparative effects of DMC tasks on IDs are strongly encouraged.

**Implications for Teachers**

In this final section, the implications of the studies reviewed in this chapter, specifically for L2 writing teachers and classroom practitioners, are discussed. The first pedagogical implication pertains to the ID of identity. Multiple studies outlined in this chapter have illustrated that various DMC tasks have the potential to serve as a positive force on aspects of L2 learners' identity development. For instance, as was demonstrated in Pyo's (2016: 427) case study of the student John, a DMC assignment such as digital storytelling enabled the young learner to 'compensate for his limitations in English', and in turn, it offered him an additional means of developing his voice and identity as an L2 writer. Relatedly, in Dávila and Susberry's (2021) study of a group of adolescent L2 English learners, the authors noted that the projects they used (i.e. posters and screenplays) appeared to help their students, who faced marginalization in society. Finally, in Jiang *et al.*'s (2020) study of an ethnic minority student in a mainstream classroom, the authors remarked how the repeated use of DMC projects emboldened their focal student to speak on class topics and on her background and knowledge of Tibetan culture, thereby making her feel increasingly positive about her ethnic identity.

As these studies suggest, it is important to note that in some cases, traditional monomodal assignments may restrict or inhibit some learners from being full participants in the L2 classroom. Although some students may actually be quite eager to participate in class discussions and assignments (and may even have a strong affinity for writing and speaking), various factors may stop them from doing so, such as their limited L2 proficiencies, the nature of the monomodal task itself and/or feeling like an outsider. Therefore, in general, L2 writing instructors should consider the extent to which their curriculum adopts multimodal writing tasks (if at all). If none is currently adopted, what is clear from the aforementioned studies is that there is a distinct possibility that some students who want to engage may ultimately decide not to do so. At minimum, it is recommended that L2 writing teachers consider implementing or experimenting with at least one multimodal writing task or DMC activity, and then examining the extent to which that activity engages different students and learner populations in their classroom. Importantly, teachers do not have to make drastic changes to their curricula in order to experiment with multimodal writing and DMC tasks. For instance, although the teachers in Jiang *et al.* (2020) used multiple digital video projects over a lengthy period of time – which is a rather sizable curriculum change – teachers might simply consider adopting a shorter activity such as storyboarding or a digital poster/advertisement. This way, teachers could first experiment with DMC within the span of only one or two class periods. As noted, this can be especially important for teachers who have diverse students from different cultural and socioeconomic backgrounds, since the adoption of one or more collaborative DMC activities may provide students with a new opportunity to express themselves and to develop increasing confidence in their identities as L2 writers.

The second pedagogical implication discussed here pertains to the ID of motivation. This implication is rather straightforward in the sense that, of those studies reviewed in this chapter, all strongly suggest that L2 learners generally find DMC tasks motivating (e.g. Hava, 2021; Henry, 2019). In some cases, students may also find them to be much more motivating than traditional monomodal writing tasks (e.g. Yang & Wu, 2012). Therefore, if not for the potential benefits that DMC tasks may have on promoting learners' identity development, writing teachers should strongly consider adopting DMC tasks for the motivational benefits. The studies in this chapter suggest that DMC tasks may be particularly engaging and motivating to L2 learners if there is some aspect of collaboration or group work involved in the project, and also if students will eventually have to share their DMC projects with the class (e.g. oral presentations) or with the general public more broadly (e.g. blogging). Thus, L2 writing teachers may wish to consider adopting a collaborative DMC project that results in students sharing and showcasing their projects within the classroom, within the school or online via a platform or social media.

Although the findings are not yet conclusive, it is also important to note that studies such as Henry (2019) suggest that teachers may need to consider additional factors when adopting collaborative DMC projects. For instance, in his study, Henry noted that there appeared to be variations in the motivational levels of different groups of students over time. While fluctuations in motivation among individual learners are by no means surprising (e.g. Campbell & Storch, 2011; Csizér, 2019), through Henry's (2019) classroom observations, he specifically linked some of these variations to differences in the groups' genders and other social factors. Therefore, this may be something that L2 writing teachers need to consider. Specifically, teachers may wish to consider assigning students to groups rather than letting students select their own groups, especially if teachers have any reservations about certain individuals/groups of students and their capacity to consistently maintain focus and motivation over a multi-week project. Thus, while DMC tasks have the capacity to motivate students, other factors must be considered.

The final pedagogical implication for classroom teachers involves the ID of metacognition. On this topic, some pedagogical insights may be gleaned from Negretti and McGrath's (2018) study of L2 writers' metacognition and genre knowledge. In their study, the researchers used a multimodal visualization reflection activity as a means of tapping into students' metacognition, and for further understanding learners' conceptualizations and awareness of different features of the target genre. Although there is still relatively limited DMC-focused scholarship on this topic, there are multiple studies on the use of visualization reflections across applied linguistics and education. In such studies that have adopted multimodal visualizations as a source of data, students are typically asked to begin by illustrating a topic, concept or something related to their learning (e.g. a process). Then, students are asked to reflect on their drawing and to describe it orally. As researchers have noted, these types of visualization reflection activities have the capacity to promote metacognition and to distill students' conceptual knowledge (Lowe & Ploetzner, 2017). Likewise, they have the capacity to be used with both adult populations (as in Negretti & McGrath, 2018) and younger children (see Winke *et al.*, 2018).

Because of these potential benefits, there are multiple ways in which L2 writing instructors might adopt multimodal visualization activities in their classrooms. The first possible use for multimodal visualizations that teachers might consider is adopting them as a pre-writing activity. Because visualization techniques can promote metacognition and help distill students' conceptual knowledge, writing teachers might implement a brief DMC visualization activity prior to having students engage in a more traditional essay-writing activity (e.g. argumentative or compare-contrast essay), especially if instructors are required to teach such essays as part of a standardized curriculum. For example, students might first be told to 'visualize what makes a successful argumentative essay', and then be asked to illustrate this using an online digital tool (see Chapter 7 for suggestions). After an appropriate amount of time (e.g. 10 minutes), students could then be asked to share their illustration with a peer and to explain what it means/represents. This sharing of ideas has the capacity to promote peer-to-peer learning and collective scaffolding. It also has the capacity to activate students' existing background knowledge prior to performing the actual essay-writing task.

The second and final way that instructors might consider using multimodal visualizations is as a means of informal assessment. For example, when teaching lengthier or more complex academic genres such as research proposals, instructors could implement a multimodal visualization activity in a similar way as described in the previous paragraph (i.e. by asking learners to visualize what makes a 'successful' piece of writing, or by articulating a certain idea or construct). However, part way through teaching such a genre, teachers could implement a multimodal visualization activity as a means of understanding their learners' current knowledge state. That is, to what extent are students able to visualize and articulate some of the key genre-related features that have been discussed in class so far, such as the audience, purpose, organization and typical rhetorical features? Relatedly, students could be asked to visualize the process of conducting research and/or finding appropriate background literature. Teachers could then walk around the classroom as students compare and discuss their multimodal visualizations. When doing so, the instructor could informally assess which areas students seem to grasp and which areas may still require additional attention in future class sessions. Thus, multimodal visualization activities can easily be implemented in the L2 writing classroom for a number of useful purposes.

# Part 3
# Pedagogical Applications

# 7 DMC Tasks and Activities

## Introduction

This chapter is the first in Part 3 of this book, which turns to a discussion of the practical pedagogical applications of the digital multimodal composing (DMC) research that was discussed in Chapters 3–6. Following this introductory section, the next section provides readers with a systematic review of popular DMC tasks and activities, including some of those less commonly used tasks that were highlighted in Chapters 3–6. In addition to the tasks discussed in this book, DMC tasks published more broadly within the domains of applied linguistics, education, computer-assisted language learning (CALL) and second language (L2) writing are reviewed. The purpose of this second expanded review is to provide a more thorough understanding of current pedagogical practices beyond those studies that have been showcased in this book. After providing an overview of commonly used tasks in L2 research, the next section of this chapter ('Options for Teachers') describes several DMC tasks in more detail, including suggestions for how instructors might implement them in various instructional contexts with learner populations of various proficiency levels. The final section ('Resources') provides a table and list of resources for teachers to further explore. Included in this section are suggestions for different digital technologies, platforms, applications and tools that can be used when adopting the DMC tasks discussed in this chapter.

## Review of Commonly Used DMC Tasks and Activities

In this section, the DMC tasks and activities that were discussed in Chapters 3–6 are reviewed. Then, a larger, more scoping review of DMC tasks is presented for comparison and for highlighting the prevalence and adoption of DMC tasks more broadly.

In this book, a total of 36 ($k = 36$) studies were reviewed in detail when discussing the topics of L2 learners' writing processes (Chapter 3), outcomes and evidence of learning (Chapter 4), teachers' and students' perceptions (Chapter 5) and individual differences such as identity, motivation and metacognition (Chapter 6). Notably, when examining the tasks and activities used in these 36 studies, one study had to be omitted from the current review (i.e. Tan & Matsuda, 2020) because the DMC task was not clearly specified in the article in terms of its aim and scope. Therefore, the DMC tasks used by authors in 35 total studies were reviewed. These data are shown in Table 7.1.

As shown in Table 7.1, researchers adopted 12 different types of DMC tasks and activities in their studies. In many cases, the researchers also served as the teachers and implemented the tasks. The majority of the studies' authors tended to adopt one of two tasks: either digital storytelling or digital videos. Together, these two DMC tasks accounted for approximately 60% of the total tasks that were used. Following the adoption of these two tasks, there is a significant drop off in terms of the popularity of other types of DMC activities. For instance, the next closest activity in terms of frequency is research proposals or essays, which were sometimes transformed into DMC assignments via the use of digital tools. They were used in 11.4% of the studies reviewed. After research proposals or essays, other DMC tasks were used, albeit infrequently. These included activities such as blogs or websites, digital booklets, infographics, digital posters, multimodal reflections or visualization reflections and slideshow presentations.

As the review shown in Table 7.1 represents a hand-selected sample of studies that focus on four specific topic areas, as mentioned, it is also

**Table 7.1** Review of DMC tasks and activities discussed in Chapters 3–6

| Name of task | No. of studies reviewed using the task | Percentage of studies reviewed using the task |
|---|---|---|
| (1) Digital storytelling | 11 | 31.4 |
| (2) Digital videos | 10 | 28.6 |
| (3) Research proposals or essays (e.g. argumentative, expository) | 4 | 11.4 |
| (4) Blogs or websites | 3 | 8.6 |
| (5) Digital booklets or infographics | 2 | 5.7 |
| (6) Digital posters | 2 | 5.7 |
| (7) Multimodal reflections or visualization reflections | 2 | 5.7 |
| (8) Slideshow presentations | 2 | 5.7 |
| (9) 3D maps | 1 | 2.9 |
| (10) Claymation | 1 | 2.9 |
| (11) Screenplays | 1 | 2.9 |
| (12) Storyboarding | 1 | 2.9 |
| Total | 40[a] | |

[a] The total number of tasks shown in the table exceeds the number of studies reviewed (i.e. $k$ = 35) because some studies adopted more than one DMC task as part of their research design.

important to survey the DMC literature to compare these findings with DMC studies that have been published more broadly on other topics in the (sub)fields of applied linguistics, education, CALL and L2 writing. Therefore, a more comprehensive review was conducted of DMC studies that were published up through the end of the 2022 calendar year (i.e. at the time this book and chapter were written).

When looking for published literature on the topic of DMC, in addition to searching for studies that were published as part of edited volumes, searches were conducted using popular academic journal databases, including Google Scholar (scholar.google.com) and the Linguistics and Language Behavior Database (LLBA; proquest.libguides.com/llba). When searching for articles via Google Scholar and the LLBA, first, a list of key search terms was created as a means of locating potential articles. These search terms included *compos\**, *digital*, *L2*, *mode*, *multimodal\**, *tech\** and *writing*. Once potential studies were located via a database, subsequent determinations needed to be made as to whether a study should be included. For example, in order for a study to be included, the primary criterion was that it had to be empirical in nature. That is, the author(s) had to have collected data surrounding the use or implementation of at least one DMC task. The study itself could not be a review article (e.g. Zhang *et al.*, 2023) or a commentary on the use of different DMC tasks (e.g. Kessler & Marino, 2023).

Following a search of the databases and after screening any/all potential studies, a total of 68 studies were found to have met these criteria. Notably, 35 of the 68 studies located are discussed in Table 7.1 (and in Chapters 3–6). This left an additional 33 studies[1] that were novel for the review. Table 7.2 shows a detailed breakdown of the different types of DMC tasks and activities that were leveraged in all 68 studies reviewed.

As illustrated in Table 7.2, among the DMC literature more broadly, both digital storytelling and digital video tasks remained the two most frequently used activities by researchers and teachers. These two tasks accounted for approximately 66% of all those DMC tasks that were adopted, which is an increase from the 60% majority that is depicted in Table 7.1. When further comparing the data from Table 7.1 with Table 7.2, a few notable differences can be seen. For one, slideshow presentation tasks appear to be used more frequently in the published literature more broadly (now moving into the #3 spot in Table 7.2). Secondly, two new types of DMC tasks are included in Table 7.2, which are not in Table 7.1. These tasks include the use of comics (Unsworth & Mills, 2020) and digital postcards (Akoto, 2021). Apart from these few differences, the types of DMC tasks discussed in this book and across the published literature more broadly appear to show relatively similar trends in terms of use and popularity.

**Table 7.2** Review of DMC tasks and activities in published studies (k = 68) from 2005 to 2022

| Name of task | No. of total studies reviewed using task | Percentage of total studies reviewed using task |
| --- | --- | --- |
| (1) Digital storytelling | 23 | 33.8 |
| (2) Digital videos | 22 | 32.4 |
| (3) Slideshow presentations | 7 | 10.3 |
| (4) Digital posters | 4 | 5.9 |
| (5) Research proposal or essays (e.g. argumentative, expository) | 4 | 5.9 |
| (6) Blogs or websites | 4 | 5.9 |
| (7) Digital booklets or infographics | 3 | 4.4 |
| (8) 3D maps | 2 | 2.9 |
| (9) Multimodal reflections or visualization reflections | 2 | 2.9 |
| (10) Claymation | 1 | 1.5 |
| (11) Comics | 1 | 1.5 |
| (12) Digital postcards | 1 | 1.5 |
| (13) Screenplays | 1 | 1.5 |
| (14) Storyboarding | 1 | 1.5 |
| Total | 76[a] | |

[a] The total number of tasks used exceeds the number of studies reviewed (i.e. 68) because some studies adopted more than one DMC task as part of their research design.

## Options for Teachers

This part of the chapter now turns to a more detailed discussion of some of the activities outlined in the previous section. Specifically, this section describes seven different types of DMC tasks, including what these tasks entail, how they might be set up by a teacher inside (or outside) of the classroom, as well as other important factors to consider when adopting these tasks. In this section, the two most popular DMC tasks highlighted in the previous literature review are discussed: digital storytelling and digital videos. Also discussed are five less commonly used tasks: 3D maps, digital posters, infographics, multimodal reflections/visualization reflections and storyboarding. The decision to include these less commonly used tasks was made for a number of reasons. For one, it is important to provide teachers with a range of options to consider in different scenarios (e.g. meeting the time they have available, and meeting the various needs and abilities of their L2 learners). For instance, although digital storytelling and digital video tasks typically take a considerable amount of time to implement due to their multi-staged nature, other DMC tasks described in what follows can be completed in a much shorter timeframe, often within one class period (e.g. digital posters) or even within 15–20 minutes (e.g. multimodal reflections/visualization reflections). Relatedly, these tasks were also selected due to the perceived feasibility (from a teacher's perspective) of both learning them and implementing them effectively. Although other DMC tasks are listed in Table 7.2, logistically speaking, some of these might be considerably challenging or far too time-consuming to implement (e.g. claymation). Additionally, other tasks were omitted because it is highly likely that teachers are already familiar with them (e.g. slideshow presentations using Microsoft PowerPoint or related software).

Next, teachers should also note that these various DMC tasks require a range of technical skills, with digital storytelling and digital video tasks likely requiring the greatest number of skills for students to complete (e.g. the capacity to record and edit images, video and sound). Moving down this broad spectrum, other DMC tasks require fewer technical skills comparatively speaking, with 3D maps, infographics, storyboarding, digital posters and multimodal reflections/visualization reflections requiring the fewest number of skills. Thus, although it is not explicitly mentioned in the description of each DMC task that follows, teachers should be aware that each task requires a slightly different level of technological literacy. Before students begin any of these tasks, instructors should set aside time to introduce their students to the necessary digital platforms and tools needed for completing the task (example tools are highlighted in the section titled 'Resources'). Teachers should also strongly consider demonstrating these tools for their students, as well as providing their learners with any additional help resources available (e.g. instructional YouTube videos, or a link to the help guide on the platform's webpage).

Finally, from a pedagogical standpoint, teachers should note that the DMC tasks described in what follows are all relatively flexible in terms of their target(s) of instruction. That is to say, because L2 instructors will undoubtedly be teaching specific content in their classrooms, teachers should think about how their target objectives (e.g. grammar points, pronunciation, vocabulary, culture) can be integrated into these DMC tasks. Thus, when describing the DMC tasks, specific linguistic foci are not addressed since they may vary widely depending on the proficiency level of the students. However, when considering the following activities, teachers should consciously think about how they can use the task as a means of eliciting the target content and linguistic forms from their students. For instance, this could be accomplished by including this information as a requirement in the assignment directions and/or grading rubric (see Chapter 8 for more on the topic of assessment with DMC).

## Digital storytelling

The first and most widely used DMC task is *digital storytelling*. As its name implies, digital storytelling is a type of multimodal narrative, and it has been used in both first language (L1) and L2 writing classrooms (Kim & Lee, 2017). Notably, there is much variation in terms of how these tasks can be adopted by instructors. For instance, the topic of the narratives that students are asked to create can be more personal in nature, in which students tell stories about their own lives and experiences (such as their daily routines, families and future career plans). However, students might also be asked to produce narratives that are less personal in nature and center instead on specific readings that are being discussed in the classroom. For example, a teacher might ask his or her students to take the point of view of a person or character in an assigned reading, and then to narrate aspects of this person's thoughts, emotions, actions and decision-making processes, thereby extending certain aspects of the completed reading.

Once the topic of the digital storytelling task has been decided upon, teachers must then consider how to go about implementing the task. Most frequently, digital storytelling tasks are adopted as multi-stage projects, which require a number of weeks to complete. For instance, in Yang *et al.* (2020), students completed a sequence of activities that built toward a final digital storytelling project. In the researchers' study, the project consisted of stages such as students brainstorming story ideas (Week 1), officially deciding on their topics (Week 2), creating storyboards (Week 3), writing scripts (Week 4), revising their scripts (Week 5), designing/creating their stories (Week 6), revising their stories (Week 7) and presenting their final digital storytelling projects to the entire class (Week 8). When designing their stories, students in Yang *et al.*'s study used digital presentation software (Prezi) and the program Audacity to orally record their narratives, which they then embedded in their digital presentation slides.

Teachers should note that depending on their own needs and the time that they have available, a digital storytelling task could easily be modified to take less (or more) time by eliminating or expanding those stages described above. Teachers could also assign some of the stages as in-class activities, while other stages could be assigned for homework outside of the classroom. Additionally, while teachers might have students create a Prezi- or PowerPoint-based multimodal composition as a base for narrating their stories, de Jager *et al.* (2017) note that instructors might also consider having students produce short video clips of between two and five minutes in length in which students combine images (or screenshots), voiceover narration and other modes. Thus, it is important to note that the central component of narration and the narrative genre always remains consistent in a digital storytelling task. Yet, there is much flexibility for instructors to modify these tasks according to their own preferences and the needs of their learners.

## Digital videos

Apart from digital storytelling, *digital video* tasks have also frequently been used by teachers and researchers in a number of instructional contexts, including both second and foreign language classrooms. Before adopting digital videos as a pedagogic activity, teachers should first note that these tasks may be somewhat similar to digital storytelling in a number of respects. For one, digital videos also typically require multiple weeks for students to complete, and they are often given as projects where students complete parts both within and beyond the walls of the classroom. Second, both digital videos and digital storytelling tasks may involve the production and recording of videos. However, digital storytelling tasks revolve around students producing narratives, but in digital videos, learners typically create videos for different purposes.

For digital video projects, instructors might begin by giving their students an assignment to craft a video on a specific topic that is being covered in class. For instance, for lower levels of L2 proficiency, topics might be related to aspects of the target country's culture (such as food, fashion, travel and climate); for higher levels of L2 proficiency, topics might involve aspects of discipline-specific research that are of interest to the students (such as those related to their major areas of study in science, engineering and literature). At this point, teachers will also give students information about the target genre and the purpose of the video. For example, learners might be asked to create a digital video in the form of a persuasive advertisement, or they might be asked to explain or describe a phenomenon in a documentary-style video. When doing so, teachers should also specify other aspects of the digital video project, such as the different stages of the project (if adopting more than one for assessment purposes). As demonstrated in a study by Chen (2018), different stages of creating a digital video might include having students (1) write scripts; (2) peer review each other's written scripts; (3) record and edit their videos to include modes such as oral speech/narration, soundtracks, images and moving video; and (4) share and comment on each other's videos on completion. Thus, again similar to digital storytelling, some of these activities might occur in the context of the classroom (e.g. stages #1 and 2), while other stages might be assigned to students as homework outside of class (e.g. stages #3 and 4).

## 3D maps

The next activity discussed is the use of *3D maps*. As the name suggests, in this DMC activity, students use a specific platform or app in order to create a digital, multidimensional map of some kind. This activity can be adopted with students of various proficiency levels, including beginner, intermediate or advanced L2 learners. In 3D map tasks, teachers typically give students an assignment in which they must create a map for visitors or tourists to a specific location or city. For instance, using an assigned app of the teacher's choosing, students might be required to create a 3D map of their school and the surrounding block/area, with the purpose of showing their maps to new students so that they can navigate the grounds (e.g. Canale, 2022). In a slight variation of this, instead, students might be asked to create a 3D map of a specific town or city, such as their hometown or another city in which people speak the target language that the students are currently learning. Regardless, when creating their maps, students are usually required to embed various multimedia into their maps so that potential users can virtually explore different aspects of the focal area or city (e.g. by clicking on different points on the map to view photos, graphics and written descriptions of places such as restaurants and other tourist attractions).

Similar to digital storytelling and digital video tasks, 3D maps usually require many weeks for students to finish. However, this may also depend on the proficiency level of the L2 learners. For instance, lower- or novice-level students may be asked to create relatively simple maps that involve only one to three targets (e.g. a single restaurant, or two or three major cultural sites), while intermediate and advanced learners may be required to create maps that are more expansive. However, in order for the project to be successful, teachers will likely need to devote multiple class periods (even for relatively simple 3D maps) or even weeks (for more complex assignments) to the activity. Creating 3D maps may consist of numerous stages, such as having students (1) plan their maps, (2) research the target sites (if necessary), (3) create and find new or existing content such as textual descriptions and images, (4) revise/edit their work and (5) share their work with their peers. Once again, similar to both digital storytelling and digital video tasks, depending on the teacher's preferences and the time available, some of these stages could be assigned during class time or for homework.

### Digital posters

The next DMC task that instructors might consider adopting in their classrooms is *digital posters*. These tasks are far less time-consuming when compared to digital storytelling, digital videos and 3D map activities. When using digital poster tasks, students are typically provided with a topic or prompt by the instructor. For example, for lower L2 proficiencies (beginner or even for intermediate levels), students might be asked to create a digital poster in which they advertise or promote something (e.g. a product, a restaurant, tourism and travel to their hometown or another focal city). For more advanced L2 learners, they might create digital posters for explanatory or informational purposes, such as discussing a current research project they are working on in another class.

Once a teacher has determined the topic and focus of the digital poster activity, the next step is to consider how the task will be implemented. One option is to have students complete the activity in class, and if the topic is not overly complex (e.g. advertising tourism to a focal city), it may be possible for students to complete their posters in as little as one or two class periods. However, for more complex tasks such as discussing one's research activities, this may work better as an out-of-class activity. Once finished, students could then subsequently share their final posters either in class or online in a poster-sharing and presentation session. Another interesting option for digital posters can be found in a study by Dzekoe (2017). Specifically, the teacher in Dzekoe's study first had the students write a traditional monomodal essay. However, students were then required to transform their monomodal essays into digital posters, integrating as many modes as they wanted. As Dzekoe noted, the goal of this transformation activity was to help students consciously notice (see Schmidt, 1990) different aspects of their writing, including any grammatical issues or gaps in their reasoning which might need further attention. Thus, as shown, when using digital posters, there are multiple ways to implement and modify them according to one's own instructional needs.

## Infographics

The fifth DMC task discussed in this section is the use of *infographics*. In many ways, infographics are similar to digital posters; however, the goal or purpose of an infographic is to take complex information and/or processes and try to convey that information in both a concise and visually appealing way. As such, this task might be somewhat difficult for students with lower levels of L2 proficiency, and it might be more suitable for intermediate- or advanced-level learners. When assigning an infographics task, like most DMC tasks, the first thing that a teacher must do is decide on the topic or area of focus. For instance, teachers might have students create an infographic as a means of explaining an aspect of history (e.g. key events or moments of a country, or the life of a specific author or historical figure). Another potential topic might involve students explaining a scientific concept or process in their field or major, breaking down all of the steps involved in it (e.g. the steps involved in a volcano erupting, or the process of photosynthesis). In an English for Academic Purposes class, students might be asked to create an infographic discussing something related to their academic lives, such as the different steps involved in conducting and writing a research paper.

When asking students to create infographics, teachers typically need to specify which modes must be integrated. Often, at a minimum, this includes linguistic text, images and colors. Because it involves taking complex information and distilling it into a reader-friendly step-by-step chart, this type of activity may best be implemented with different components completed in and out of class, respectively. For instance, if the topic is not assigned by the teacher, then teachers might have students brainstorm potential topics and discuss them in class. Students could also draft and outline the steps they might include during class. However, because the design portion will likely take some time to complete, students could do this for homework over one to two weeks. Similar to digital posters, once completed, students could then share their final infographics in class or online.

### Multimodal reflections/visualization reflections

The sixth option for a DMC activity discussed here is the use of *multimodal reflections/visualization reflections* (hereafter referred to as 'multimodal visualizations'). Of all the activities described in this section, this activity takes the least amount of time to complete. Depending on a teacher's goal as well, this activity could be completed in as few as 15–20 minutes. In a multimodal visualization, teachers ask their students to visualize and illustrate a concept, idea or process. For instance, for students with lower levels of L2 proficiency, they might be asked to visualize and illustrate the different verb tenses that they are learning in class (by combining images, colors and written linguistic text). Another option is to ask students to illustrate what they think makes a good argumentative paragraph (or whatever target essay form students are currently learning). For higher levels of L2 proficiency, as was adopted in an article by Negretti and McGrath (2018), students might be asked to illustrate their knowledge of a specific genre (e.g. their knowledge of the research article genre). After producing their multimodal visualization, students are then typically asked to describe the visuals that they produced either to another student or to the teacher, including what each component represents.

Notably, multimodal visualizations can be used in a myriad of ways in the L2 classroom. For instance, one possible way is to use multimodal visualizations as a pre-task activity. Since visualizations have the capacity to promote metacognition and to consolidate learners' conceptual knowledge, this makes them suitable to use before any number of tasks (e.g. a writing or a speaking activity). They can be used as a means of activating students' existing background knowledge and helping them think about the purpose of the task itself, the key vocabulary needed for performing the task and more. Apart from this possible use, another way that teachers might consider using multimodal visualizations is for informal needs assessment purposes. For example, prior to teaching a specific genre or topic, teachers might ask their L2 learners to produce a multimodal visualization (e.g. on the key components of writing an effective summary). Afterward, as students are sharing their visualizations with a partner, the teacher could walk around the room and take note of the common themes in those comments made by students, thereby informally assessing students' existing knowledge of the topic. Relatedly, rather than being adopted as a needs assessment prior to teaching, instructors might also use multimodal visualizations as a type of ongoing assessment in order to see what aspects (despite already being covered) may require extra attention.

## Storyboarding

The seventh and final DMC task described here is the use of *storyboarding*. Many teachers are likely familiar with a common classroom activity that is similar to storyboarding, which is the use of picture description activities. However, unlike picture description activities in which the instructor typically gives the students a set of images from which to work, with storyboarding, the students must create both the narrative story *and* produce the illustrations themselves (i.e. by virtually drawing or integrating existing images, video and/or sound). Like picture description activities, in storyboarding, each visual is accompanied by linguistic text that helps narrate or advance the story and explain what is happening in the image. Storyboarding activities can be done with lower-level L2 learners (e.g. storyboarding and narrating their daily activities from morning to evening), along with intermediate- and advanced-level L2 learners (e.g. storyboarding major events in a reading they completed as part of class).

Like some digital poster activities, storyboarding tasks can likely be completed in as little as one or two class periods, depending on how many frames an instructor asks students to illustrate and narrate in the activity. Typically, storyboarding templates will include anywhere from four to eight frames. Also of note is that storyboarding activities can be used simply as a one-off activity, as was described in the previous paragraph. However, as noted in some of the descriptions of earlier DMC tasks such as digital storytelling and digital videos, storyboarding can also be used as a planning activity that students engage in prior to shooting and editing digital videos. Thus, instructors have multiple options in terms of integrating storyboarding into their L2 teaching practices.

## Resources

This final section of the chapter provides L2 writing teachers and other practitioners with a list of potential resources. Specifically, based on the various DMC tasks and activities reviewed in Tables 7.1 and 7.2, Table 7.3 provides teachers with a list of examples for different digital platforms, tools and apps that they might consider exploring when implementing the aforementioned DMC activities. Table 7.3 lists the

**Table 7.3** DMC tasks and potential platforms, tools and apps for implementation

| Name of task | Name of platform/tool/site | Link to learn more |
|---|---|---|
| 3D maps | • 3D-mapper [F]<br>• Icograms [F]<br>• Maps3D<br>• SketchUp | • 3d-mapper.com<br>• icograms.com<br>• maps3d.io<br>• sketchup.com |
| Blogs or websites | • Blogger [F]<br>• Google Sites [F]<br>• Weebly [F]<br>• WordPress [F] | • blogger.com<br>• sites.google.com<br>• weebly.com<br>• wordpress.com |
| Comics | • Canva [F]<br>• Pixton [F]<br>• Smilebox [F] | • canva.com<br>• pixton.com<br>• smilebox.com |
| Digital postcards | • Canva [F]<br>• Visme [F]<br>• VistaCreate [F] | • canva.com<br>• visme.co<br>• create.vista.com |
| Digital posters | • Adobe Express [F]<br>• Canva [F]<br>• Microsoft PowerPoint<br>• Venngage [F] | • adobe.com<br>• canva.com<br>• microsoft.com<br>• venngage.com |
| Digital storytelling | • Canva [F]<br>• iMovie<br>• Microsoft PowerPoint<br>• Prezi<br>• Storybird<br>• VivaVideo [F] | • canva.com<br>• apple.com<br>• microsoft.com<br>• prezi.com<br>• storybird.com<br>• vivavideo.tv |
| Digital videos | • Filmora [F]<br>• Final Cut Pro<br>• iMovie<br>• Movie Maker Online [F] | • filmora.wondershare.net<br>• apple.com/final-cut-pro<br>• apple.com<br>• moviemakeronline.com |
| Infographics | • Adobe Express [F]<br>• Canva [F]<br>• Venngage [F]<br>• Visme [F] | • adobe.com<br>• canva.com<br>• venngage.com<br>• visme.co |
| Multimodal reflections or visualization reflections | • Google Drawings [F]<br>• Kleki [F]<br>• Sketchpad [F]<br>• Web Whiteboard [F] | • docs.google.com<br>• kleki.com<br>• sketch.io<br>• webwhiteboard.com |
| Research proposals/essays (e.g. argumentative, expository) | • Google Docs [F]<br>• Nuclino [F]<br>• SlimWiki [F] | • docs.google.com<br>• nuclino.com<br>• slimwiki.com |
| Screenplays | • Arc Studio Pro [F]<br>• Celtx<br>• Writer Duet [F] | • arcstudiopro.com<br>• celtx.com<br>• writerduet.com |

(Continued)

**Table 7.3** (Continued)

| Name of task | Name of platform/tool/site | Link to learn more |
|---|---|---|
| Slideshow presentations | • Canva [F]<br>• Google Slides [F]<br>• Microsoft PowerPoint<br>• Prezi | • canva.com<br>• google.com<br>• microsoft.com<br>• prezi.com |
| Storyboarding | • Canva [F]<br>• Milanote [F]<br>• Storybird<br>• StoryboardThat | • canva.com<br>• milanote.com<br>• storybird.com<br>• storyboardthat.com |

Note: Platforms with superscript 'F' were either free or had multiple features that could be used for free at the time this chapter was written.

names of the focal DMC task (e.g. blogs), the names of multiple available digital platforms and tools (e.g. Blogger, Google Sites, Weebly and WordPress) and a corresponding web link where interested readers can learn more about each resource.

When compiling this list of resources, it is important to note that attempts have been made to include at least three potential options for each DMC task. This includes providing platforms that are freely available to teachers and their students and those that are available only through paid subscription. All free options are indicated in the table by superscript 'F', which appears to the right of the platform or application's name. Additionally, readers should note that the 'Link to learn more' column in Table 7.3 includes a link to the platform's main homepage. For instance, for the DMC task of digital posters, the platform Canva is one of the available options listed, and the web link appears in the table as *canva.com*. This link does not take users directly to the part of Canva's site that is devoted to digital posters; however, users should be able to easily find the DMC templates for digital posters by searching Canva's main page and/or by simply conducting a basic web search with the terms 'Canva' and 'digital poster template'. The decision not to include extended URLs was made because (a) sometimes these direct links may change over time and (b) the links for some of the platforms are quite lengthy.

Lastly, a final note pertains to the rationale as to why the various platforms in Table 7.3 were selected for inclusion. When possible, I have tried to include those platforms or apps that either I and/or colleagues have had experience using in the past. In some instances, platforms have also been highlighted because they were specifically mentioned by authors in the literature reviews that are shown in Tables 7.2 and 7.3. Finally, when able, I have also tried to include platforms that have how-to or help guide videos posted on their webpages, which showcase the different features that are available, along with how to use and navigate them.

## Note

(1) The 33 additional studies added to the review in Table 7.2 include Abdel-Hack and Helwa (2014), Akoto (2021), Azis and Mataram (2020), Balaman (2018), Canale (2022), Castañeda *et al.* (2018), Engin (2014), Hafner (2015), Hafner and Ho (2020), Hafner and Miller (2011), Huang (2022), Hung *et al.* (2013), Jiang (2018), Jiang and Gao (2020), Jiang and Luk (2016), Jiang and Ren (2021), Jiang *et al.* (2022), Kim and Lee (2017), Lee *et al.* (2021), Liang (2019), Nelson (2006), Ørevik (2022), Oskoz and Elola (2016), Park (2021), Priego and Liaw (2017), Schrieber (2015), Tardy (2005), Towndrow *et al.* (2013), Unsworth and Mills (2020), Yeh (2018), Yeh and Mitric (2019), Yi and Angay-Crowder (2016), Zhang and O'Halloran (2019).

# 8 Assessment

**Introduction**

Thus far, this book has centered on discussing a small number of key areas pertaining to digital multimodal composing (DMC) within the domain of second language acquisition (SLA). This includes topics on the key theories and concepts that have motivated DMC's general use (Chapter 2), how scholars have researched DMC's influence on various aspects of second language (L2) learning both inside and outside of the classroom (Chapters 3–6) and also the types of DMC tasks, activities and tools that are available for instructors to use in practice (Chapter 7). Clearly, DMC has much support both in terms of theory and published research, and there are also a plethora of activities that teachers can adopt. However, one lingering question that many teachers (and researchers) might have pertains to the topic of assessment. The question is: How does one actually go about assessing a student's DMC product that contains multiple modes, including those that are linguistic, visual, oral, gestural and/or spatial in nature? Admittedly, of all the areas covered throughout this book and across the published literature more broadly, the topic of assessment has received the least amount of attention. This speaks to the relative difficulty of assessing DMC to date, particularly in fields such as applied linguistics, SLA and L2 writing, where traditionally, decades of research and pedagogy have been devoted to developing a set of best practices for assessing L2 learners' linguistic output in the forms of oral and written language only (see Winke and Brunfaut [2021] for a comprehensive review of topics and issues involving language testing).

In an effort to further develop teachers' understanding of this important area, this chapter covers the topic of assessment and DMC. To better facilitate the nexus between theory, research and practice, the next section provides readers with a brief overview of some of the key literature that has explored issues pertaining to DMC assessment. The rest of the chapter focuses on describing particular studies in detail, which have concrete pedagogical implications for assessing L2 learners' DMC products. This includes pedagogical tips and recommendations for adopting a *product-based* approach for assessing learners' DMC projects or for adopting a *process-based* approach for assessment purposes. Finally, similar to Chapter 7, which covered a range of DMC tasks and activities, this chapter concludes with a list of digital platforms, tools and other resources that teachers might consider using for assessment purposes.

## Literature Review of Research on Assessment and DMC

As has been noted by numerous educators, both the consumption and the teaching of digital and multimodal genres have become a widespread practice (e.g. Lim & Polio, 2020; New London Group, 1996). This includes multimodal genres being integrated into K-12 and university curricula at the local and national levels; relatedly, multimodal genres have now become an integral part of the L2 testing practices of private testing companies, in-house school-based language assessments and even national testing (Mitsikopoulou, 2022; Sindoni *et al.*, 2022). Despite the prevalence of multiple modes and multimodal genres in language testing, more often than not, test creators themselves still treat various modes in isolation and as being unimportant and only of supplemental relevance (Canale, 2022). For instance, researchers such as Campoy-Cubillo and Querol-Julián (2022) have stated that many established, internationally recognized proficiency testing bodies such as the *Common European Framework of Reference for Languages* (CEFR) have recognized multiliteracies as important for L2 learning and the development of communicative competence; however, testing is still typically geared toward one mode only, when in fact, it should be multimodal in scope. This is important because, as Jewitt (2003: 84) has remarked, 'if learning is multimodal and assessment is restricted to the modes of speech and writing the assessment will ignore (and in the process negate) much of what is learnt'.

In recent years, researchers within applied linguistics, SLA and education have begun to examine this issue more closely, with a number of exploratory studies investigating how L2 learners' DMC projects can be assessed, especially by practicing language teachers in both English as a second language (ESL) and English as a foreign language (EFL) classrooms. In terms of what has been done, most research has tended to focus on *product-based* assessments, or looking at ways to assess the final DMC products that are produced by students via the use of specific criteria and different types of rubrics. For instance, prior studies have explored the use of rubrics for assessing slideshow presentations (e.g. Hung *et al.*, 2013), rubrics for multimodal posters (e.g. Ørevik, 2022), genre-based models of assessment (e.g. Jiang *et al.*, 2022) or more formative and informal student-directed approaches to assessment (e.g. Canale, 2022). Notably, such studies can be viewed as a direct response to work by Yi *et al.* (2017), in which the authors called for digital multimodal literacy to be further developed and conceptualized. In their article, Yi and her colleagues specifically encouraged L2 writing teachers to both use and reflect upon rubrics that cover not only linguistic modes, but also content and other design aspects involved in creating DMC tasks (e.g. how the composer manipulates other modes such as images, text and sound to achieve different communicative purposes).

Although most studies involving assessment and DMC to date have tended to focus on establishing specific criteria or rubrics for assessing learners' DMC products once the composing process is complete (i.e. a product-based approach), in another study by Hafner and Ho (2020), the authors opted for a different approach. In their article, Hafner and Ho explored the adoption of a *process-based* model of assessment, in which L2 learners' DMCs were assessed at multiple stages throughout the act of composing rather than at only one point in time at the end. Because both product- and process-based models of assessment have certain strengths and weaknesses, the aforementioned articles are discussed in more depth in the following section. When doing so, the context and purpose of each study are briefly explained for the reader. However, most of the focus is dedicated to explaining the assessment process and the rubric (if applicable), along with describing how L2 writing instructors might similarly adopt these assessment models in their own classrooms.

## Recommendations for Assessing Students' DMC Projects

### Product-based assessment

As discussed in the previous section, to date, most studies involving DMC and the topic of assessment have tended to focus on *product*-based assessment. This means that teachers (and researchers) typically do not engage in assessing the focal group of L2 learners while they are in the act of designing their DMC projects. Instead, the assessments occur at the end stage, and they focus on examining the final DMC product that the students have created.

One of the first studies in this area is Hung *et al.* (2013). In the opening to their article, the authors noted that slideshow presentations have now become a staple of academic and educational practices, which are important for students to learn. Despite this, little research (at the time) had explored how such DMC products might be assessed, especially from a multiliteracies perspective (New London Group, 1996: 402). As such, the authors explored what they called a 'theory-driven design rubric', which was based on the theory of multiliteracies. The rubric itself was created for the purpose of assessing L2 English learners' slideshow presentations at a university in Taiwan. The authors called their study an action research project since the lead researcher also served as the instructor for the focal course. The creation of the rubric was carefully guided by the New London Group's

(1996) paper on multiliteracies, and specifically, the rubric aimed to assess five different modes: auditory, gestural, linguistic, spatial and visual modes. When considering these five different modes and design elements, Hung *et al.* (2013) developed a corresponding set of evaluation questions for each mode. For instance, when assessing the *linguistic* design mode, sample evaluation questions included 'Was the linguistic content comprehensible without major grammatical errors?' and 'Was the linguistic content structured in a logical and organized manner?' (2013: 402). As another example, in order to assess the *visual* design mode, some evaluation questions included 'Did the author carefully design the use of color and typology to reflect the selected visual theme?' and 'If chosen to use, did the author make meaningful use of available visual elements, such as graphics, to construct meaning in a cohesive manner?' (Hung *et al.*, 2013: 402). For the three other modal design elements (i.e. gestural, auditory and spatial modes), there were also specific evaluation questions. To see the entire evaluation rubric and list of questions, readers are encouraged to view the original article (specifically, see Hung *et al.*, 2013: 402).

Using these questions as a guide, Hung *et al.* (2013) then used a 5-point Likert scale to rate each of the modal categories as a whole in terms of their cohesion (5 = excellent, 4 = good, 3 = average, 2 = weak and 1 = poor). Students in the focal class were shown this rubric prior to composing their slideshow presentations, and after the project ended, the authors used a combination of surveys and semi-structured interviews to understand the students' opinions of the rubric. In terms of its utility, the students reported that the design rubric helped them improve their awareness of multimodal composing in general, and also to improve their ability to arrange elements when designing their projects. Importantly, the teacher (and the research team) also felt that the rubric provided them with 'a practical, holistic way to measure student performance based on the five established modes of multimodal text design' (Hung *et al.*, 2013: 408). In closing, the authors remarked that their design rubric might also be used in other creative ways, such as for self-assessment or for peer review purposes.

Similar to the study by Hung *et al.* (2013), Ørevik (2022) was motivated by a multiliteracies perspective to create a new rubric. However, Ørevik was interested in exploring the creation of a rubric for assessing the multimodal/digital posters genre. Like Hung *et al.*, Ørevik's research was also classified as an action research study. The study itself centered around a two-week long DMC project that took place with 15 L2 English learners (ages 16–17) in a Norwegian upper secondary school. For the project, the students worked either individually or in pairs to create digital posters. The purpose of the assignment was argumentative in nature, and students were supposed to convince their peers of a particular viewpoint (e.g. why the smoking and drinking age should be raised to 21).

Prior to engaging in the DMC task, students were shown an assessment rubric for their digital posters.

Ørevik's (2022) assessment rubric consisted of four different aspects:

(1) '**Relation between modes**: images and writing agreeing (or purposefully conflicting) in ways that emphasized the message…
(2) **Coherence and clarity**: clear, coherent communication in line with the communicative purpose of the genre…
(3) **Intertextuality**: textual or cultural references supporting the message…
(4) **Originality and creativity**: an inventive, creative approach to the text production…' (Ørevik, 2022: 262; bold font in original)

These four categories were then rated by the classroom instructor according to three levels: *high*, *middle* or *minimum*. Each of these three levels also had additional descriptions to help clarify what the instructor was seeking. For instance, under the fourth category of originality and creativity, the descriptors were *high* 'takes an independent and inventive approach to the text creation', *middle* 'the text creation is relatively independent, with some degree of "personal touch"' (Ørevik, 2022: 267) and *minimum* 'the text creation is "bland" with few signs of independence or creativity' (Ørevik, 2022: 268).

As mentioned, the students were shown the rubric prior to designing their digital posters, and afterward, the students also engaged in peer review with some of their classmates' posters. Following peer review and the instructor's own personal use of the rubric, Ørevik (2022) reflected upon its utility. The author noted that the rubric appeared to be a relatively effective tool for assessing digital posters. In closing, Ørevik remarked that future teachers might consider experimenting with the rubric in their own classrooms. Additionally, the author also suggested that teachers might adopt the rubric as a means of promoting students' genre awareness by having them review it both before and during the composing process.

As suggested in Ørevik's (2022) study, the concept of genre is an important consideration when assessing some (if not most) types of DMC projects. This is especially true for those digital multimodal genres that have established conventions, which may be used by learners in other academic or professional contexts (e.g. digital posters, infographics and slideshow presentations). This notion of genre as an integral part of DMC assessment is also reflected in a study by Jiang *et al.* (2022). As Jiang *et al.* (2022: 2) noted, although genre has had tremendous value in L2 writing research and pedagogy, it has been relatively 'undertheorized and underexplored' for the purposes of DMC assessment. As such, Jiang *et al.* attempted to examine the development of a genre-based model of assessment for DMC. To do so, they designed a two-stage study. In the first stage, they developed the framework for their genre-based assessment rubric. In the second stage, the researchers piloted their rubric through an action research study, in which they gave the rubric to five L2 English teachers at a university in China, who subsequently used and provided feedback on their experiences with the rubric.

For the rubric, Jiang *et al.* (2022) drew upon an existing model of genre and multimodality that was constructed by Bateman (2008), and they also drew upon key concepts from major genre theories such as the New Rhetoric/Rhetorical Genre Studies approach (e.g. Miller, 1984) and English for Specific Purposes (e.g. Swales, 1990, 2004) (for a comprehensive discussion of genre-based theories and approaches, see Kessler and Polio [2024a, 2024b]). The rubric that they ultimately drafted consisted of four major components: *base units*, *layout*, *navigation* and *rhetoric*. *Base* consisted of students' use of different modal features and selections such as the linguistic content (e.g. sentences, vocabulary), images, audio, video and color; *layout* referred to students' combination of modes and how they attempted to creatively group them together in their composition; *navigation* referred to the extent to which students were able to present information in a clear, organized and logical manner; and *rhetoric* consisted of students' appropriate use of rhetorical structures to support the target genre (e.g. using effective arguments in an argumentative genre).

Notably, unlike the other studies reviewed in this chapter thus far, Jiang *et al.*'s (2022) genre-based model of assessment was not confined to one specific DMC genre. Because of this, the teachers in their study used the model rubric in their respective classrooms for a variety of task types (e.g. digital videos and digital posters). Following the teachers' use and review of the rubric in their own courses, the teachers reported that they generally found it to be useful. However, the teachers also felt that further modifications were necessary in order to improve it. In particular, the instructors felt that the concept of *purpose* (i.e. the rationale for producing the genre) should be a key component added to the assessment model. Therefore, Jiang *et al.* present readers with a modified sample rubric for assessing DMC genres at the end of the study, with five total categories to be assessed: *purpose, base units, layout, navigation* and *rhetoric*. The authors suggest that each of these five categories could be rated by teachers using a 4-point scale, such as rating them as outstanding, good, satisfactory or failed. Like Ørevik's (2022) proposed rubric, Jiang *et al.* (2022: 6) also provide detailed descriptors to help guide teachers in making determinations of what constitutes a rating of outstanding, good, satisfactory or failed. Thus, in closing, Jiang *et al.* encourage teachers to experiment with their genre-based rubric for assessing a variety of learners' DMC products.

The final study discussed in this section on product-based assessment is Canale (2022). In the study, the author investigated a teacher's formative assessment practices in a beginner-level EFL classroom in Uruguay.

As Canale noted, the purpose of a formative assessment is for teachers to assess how a learner is progressing during the course, and to encourage and promote continued learning practices. Canale observed an L2 English teacher's class, in which the teacher gave students a DMC assignment to produce a 3D map. The project was called 'My Neighborhood' (Canale, 2022: 210), and the students were taught to use specific software that was demoed for them (called Sketchup). The students were asked to produce a 3D map of their school block and the surrounding area, including video, audio, text and images. On completion of their projects, the students then posted their 3D maps on YouTube and shared them with the entire class so that their peers and the teacher had the opportunity to navigate the school using the maps they had created. Of note is that unlike the three previous studies by Jiang *et al*. (2022), Ørevik (2022) and Hung *et al*. (2013), the focal teacher in Canale's study did not use a rubric for the purpose of grading students' DMC projects.

In terms of assessment, the focal teacher, named Vera, adopted a means of formative 'interactive assessment' (Canale, 2022: 212). At the end of the project, as students shared their presentations/tutorials, Vera engaged students by asking them multiple questions pertaining to the design of their projects. Examples of these questions included: 'How did you decide what (image, text, object, etc.) to include/exclude? What does this (image, text, object, etc.) do here? Why did you choose X (pointing to a particular object, image, etc.)?' and 'What are the differences between your text and your classmate's text?' (Canale, 2022: 211). As Canale (2022: 212) noted, the teacher favored this type of product-based formative assessment because it 'allowed the learner to demonstrate his agency', and it also enabled the students 'a means of negotiating the curriculum' (Canale, 2022: 213) by further reflecting on why they ultimately made certain decisions. Thus, Canale's study is interesting because it represents an alternative option for product-based assessment by showing an example of how questioning students' decision-making processes can be an interactive and informal means of DMC assessment, which occurs at the tail end of a project.

In terms of product-based assessment, the studies reviewed in this section can be a good starting point for teachers to consider. In the field of L2 writing, in recent years, there has been a move away from product-based writing assessment, with increased emphasis on stressing the importance of the writing process itself (see the next section and Chapter 3). However, the various forms of product-based assessment described in this section do have a number of strengths. Firstly, if teachers have large class sizes, then logistically, it may be quite challenging to engage in the type of process-based assessment described in the next section. Secondly, with the exception of Canale's (2022) study, the other studies described in this chapter were all action research oriented in nature, meaning that it was actual classroom teachers who were reflecting on the process of implementing rubrics in their own instructional contexts. Thus, if teachers are attempting to assess similar DMC tasks and activities such as slideshow presentations or digital posters, then they may wish to use the rubrics and recommendations provided by Hung *et al.* (2013) or Ørevik (2022) as a guide. Obviously, teachers can also modify these rubrics in order to meet their own needs and objectives.

Apart from these rubrics, which were created for specific DMC task types, teachers can also use Jiang *et al.*'s (2022) genre-based model and rubric as a useful guide. As noted, this rubric might be used for a variety of DMC genres and task types. It might also be especially useful if students are being asked to create a multimodal genre that has relatively established conventions by a certain audience or readership (e.g. multimodal posters for an academic conference presentation). While Jiang *et al.* did not describe the specific numerical values or points associated with each category of their rubric, teachers can easily turn this rubric into an analytic rubric by assigning specific point values. For instance, Jiang *et al.*'s rubric had five categories (e.g. rhetoric), which were then rated by teachers using the scale of outstanding, good, satisfactory and failed. This scale could be assigned a specific numerical value (e.g. outstanding = 3 points, good = 2, satisfactory = 1 and failed = 0). Similarly, teachers could also assign a range of values to this scale (e.g. outstanding = 10–9 points, good = 8–6, satisfactory = 7–4 and failed = 3–0) should they so desire.

Finally, Canale's (2022) study is worth commenting on because it showcases a means of informal formative assessment. That is, some teachers may wish to assign shorter types of DMC tasks and activities, which take relatively little time to complete (e.g. multimodal visualization reflections or storyboarding). Teachers may wish to use these as part of their regular classroom activities rather than as a larger project that is formally assessed for a grade. In such cases, Canale's study shows how teachers can still assess L2 learners' multiliteracies and their decision-making practices, and also how teachers can do so in a way that encourages interaction, critical reflection and continued learning. In sum, the product-based assessment options provided in this chapter allow for much flexibility on the part of the teacher.

## Process-based assessment

In contrast to a product-based approach, some teachers and researchers have advocated for a *process*-based approach to assessment. This focus on assessing aspects of L2 learners' writing processes reflects a broader shift in the practices of many writing educators over the past 30 years. As discussed in Chapter 3, a number of educators have tended to place less importance on students' final written compositions. Unquestionably, the final product itself is still deemed to be important; however, a process-based approach stresses the value of the entire writing process – from brainstorming, outlining, drafting and revising to finalizing one's work – with composing regarded as a lengthy, iterative process that involves multiple stages of working, reflecting and reworking one's text.

One study that exemplifies this process-based approach to DMC assessment is Hafner and Ho (2020). In their study, the authors took an exploratory approach to investigating a process-based model of DMC assessment. Their study was set in the context of an EFL science course at a university in Hong Kong. In this instructional context, the teachers were required to assign a digital video project (i.e. a scientific documentary) to their L2 English learners. For the digital video project, students were required to complete multiple stages, including: '1) reading/data collection; 2) scripting/storyboarding; 3) performing/recording; 4) editing; and 5) sharing' (Hafner & Ho, 2020: 3). Hafner and Ho noted that in the EFL program, traditionally, the digital video project was assessed in two ways. The first assessment occurred during the final video-sharing session, when students answered questions from other students, and students were also assessed by their teacher who used a rubric that was designed for the project. The rubric that the teacher used consisted of three categories: (1) *organization and content*, (2) *multimedia and visual effects* and (3) *language*, and each category was subsequently rated as outstanding, good, satisfactory, marginal or failed. In terms of the second assessment, students submitted a final reflective report in which they recounted the process of creating and designing their videos. Thus, as Hafner and Ho (2020: 4) noted, 'in this way, the assessment focuse[d] on both the DMC process and its product'.

Although this assessment process had been put in place previously, Hafner and Ho (2020) wanted to better understand how teachers perceived it from their own vantage points, including both (a) the different criteria that teachers applied when assessing students' digital videos and (b) the types of practical issues that teachers encountered when trying to grade students' work. To accomplish this, Hafner and Ho interviewed seven teachers who had taught the course during the previous two years, and these teachers shared examples of high- and low-rated digital videos they had rated using the rubric. Despite the fact that the rubric only included three categories, Hafner and Ho reported that the teachers tended to apply a total of seven criteria when assessing students' digital videos. These criteria consisted of: '1) creativity and originality, 2) organization, 3) language, 4) delivery, 5) modal interaction, 6) variety, and 7) genre' (Hafner & Ho, 2020: 10). These criteria have already been discussed to some extent in the prior studies reviewed in this chapter, so they will not be elaborated on here. However, in terms of difficulties, some of the teachers stated that the biggest challenge they faced was attempting to consider multiple modes simultaneously (i.e. primarily item #5, which involved modal interaction). This meant that teachers had to rewind and rewatch students' videos multiple times in order to analyze the use of different modal resources.

Based on their findings, Hafner and Ho (2020) suggested that teachers might consider adopting a process-based model of assessment for DMC, as this may have the capacity to address some of the challenges they faced. Although their original assessment practices included two stages, Hafner and Ho suggested expanding them to include assessment during four main stages: (1) pre-design, (2) design, (3) sharing and (4) reflecting. Importantly, the authors note that this process can involve a combination of formative assessment and summative assessment. For example, in terms of formative assessment, this might occur at the earlier stages involving the pre-design and design of the activity; yet, summative assessment might be used at the end of the DMC project during the sharing and reflection stages. Hafner and Ho (2020: 12) close their article by recommending this process-based approach because, as they note, it allows for 'work collaboratively throughout the different stages of the design process so that students receive an appropriate amount of scaffolding to develop multimodal communicative competence and digital skills'.

For L2 writing teachers, one of the main strengths of this process-based approach to assessment is the scaffolding that can be provided both by the teacher and by one's peers. This combination of formative and summative assessment, as referenced by Hafner and Ho (2020), also has the capacity to prompt students to think more critically about their decision-making processes throughout the entirety of the writing process. Practically speaking, in terms of how these assessments might occur, in the pre-design phase of a project, students will likely produce artifacts such as mind maps, storyboards or written outlines, which might then be reviewed and examined for informal assessment purposes (e.g. by the teacher and/or by other students). During the actual design phase, teachers might ask students to consider prompting questions such as those found in Canale (2022). If possible, teachers might even walk around the classroom and ask students some of these questions, while students are actively designing their DMC projects.

Next, for the sharing stage, assessment could occur through peer review, and students could then be given an opportunity to make final modifications to their projects before submitting them for a grade. At the final reflection stage, students could also craft narratives (e.g. in writing or via the creation of a short digital video) in which they reflect on the process of designing their DMC projects. This is also when the teacher might formally use a rubric for the purpose of assigning a grade, and students' reflections could even be included as part of the final assignment itself. For example, they could be included as a small percentage or completion grade of the project as a whole.

As many teachers will notice, this type of process-based assessment has clear strengths. However, teachers will also note that process-based assessment is far more involved in terms of planning and what is required on the part of the teacher. Relatedly, a process-based model of DMC assessment might prove difficult to implement if teachers have large classroom sizes. With large classrooms, it may still be possible to implement a modified version of this process-based model (e.g. by only assessing two different stages rather than all four). However, a process-based assessment is likely to be more conducive to smaller classes with 20 or fewer students.

## Resources and Tools for Assessing Students' DMC Products and Processes

As discussed throughout the chapter, when it comes to the topic of DMC assessment, there are a number of potential options, which typically fall into one of two categories involving product-based or process-based assessment. Regardless of the approach that teachers take with their students, one thing that all teachers must do is be sure to set clear expectations at the outset for their learners regarding both what will be assessed and how it will be assessed. This includes identifying the specific modes (e.g. linguistic text, images, video, soundtracks) that students must integrate into their DMC projects. This also includes explicitly telling students about the other criteria by which their DMCs will be assessed. For many studies discussed in this chapter, this may consist of areas that are designated on a corresponding rubric that cover topics of genre, rhetoric, creativity, organization, modal interaction or additional areas. As such, before one's learners ever begin the pre-task or planning phase of their assignment, teachers should show students the rubric that they will use for grading purposes, and teachers should also discuss any relevant stages in the assessment process (particularly if they are adopting a process-based approach).

The final section closes the chapter with a list of resources and tools that can be used for assessment purposes. Notably, many of these assessment resources have been discussed in this chapter in considerable detail (e.g. rubrics) or referenced only in passing (e.g. peer review). Table 8.1 showcases a number of resources for assessing L2 learners' DMC products and processes, which range from the creation of rubrics, to the pre-design phase, the sharing phase and the reflecting phase. One important note is that although *design* is listed as a phase in Hafner and Ho's (2020) article, specific design platforms, tools and technologies were previously discussed in detail in Chapter 7. Therefore, instead of repeating that information here, readers are referred to Chapter 7 for the purpose of getting ideas for designing different types of DMC tasks and activities.

Finally, similar to Chapter 7, I note that when compiling the list of resources for this chapter, I have tried to include several possible options for each type or stage of DMC assessment. This includes providing a variety of platforms that are freely available to teachers and their students, along with those that are available through paid subscription only. In Table 8.1, all free options are marked by superscript 'F' (i.e. [F]). Lastly, readers should note that in the 'Link to learn more' column in Table 8.1,

**Table 8.1** Resources and tools for assessing students' DMC products and processes

| Assessment stage | Name of resource or site | Link to learn more |
|---|---|---|
| Example rubrics | • Hafner and Ho (2020)<br>• Hung et al. (2013)<br>• Jiang et al. (2022)<br>• Ørevik (2022) | • https://doi.org/10.1016/j.jslw.2020.100710<br>• https://doi.org/10.1111/j.1467-8535.2012.01337.x<br>• https://doi.org/10.1016/j.jslw.2022.100869<br>• taylorfrancis.com (ebook ISBN: 9781003155300) |
| Rubric creation | • iRubric [F]<br>• Microsoft Excel<br>• Microsoft Word<br>• Quick Rubric [F]<br>• RubiStar [F]<br>• Rubric Maker [F] | • rcampus.com<br>• microsoft.com<br>• microsoft.com<br>• quickrubric.com<br>• rubistar.4teachers.org<br>• rubric-maker.com |
| Pre-design | • Canva [F]<br>• Lucidspark [F]<br>• Milanote [F]<br>• Mindmeister [F]<br>• Mindmup [F]<br>• Storybird<br>• StoryboardThat | • canva.com<br>• lucidspark.com<br>• milanote.com<br>• mindmeister.com<br>• mindmup.com<br>• storybird.com<br>• storyboardthat.com |
| Design | • See Chapter 7 | • See Chapter 7 for a list of sample platforms, software, tools and corresponding links for designing different types of DMC tasks and activities |
| Sharing | • Blogger [F]<br>• Google Classroom [F]<br>• Google Sites [F]<br>• Moodle [F]<br>• WeChat [F]<br>• Weebly [F]<br>• WordPress [F]<br>• YouTube [F] | • blogger.com<br>• edu.google.com<br>• sites.google.com<br>• moodle.org<br>• wechat.com<br>• weebly.com<br>• wordpress.com<br>• youtube.com |
| Reflecting | • Flipgrid [F]<br>• Google Drawings [F]<br>• Google Forms [F]<br>• Kleki [F]<br>• Microsoft Word<br>• Padlet [F] | • info.flip.com<br>• docs.google.com<br>• google.com<br>• kleki.com<br>• microsoft.com<br>• padlet.com |

Note: Resources with superscript 'F' were either free or had multiple features that could be used for free at the time this chapter was written.

I have opted to include a link to the platform's main homepage. This decision not to include extended URLs was once again made since (a) sometimes these direct links may change over time and (b) the direct links for some of the platforms are too lengthy to include in the table. However, readers should be easily able to find the specific resources they need by visiting each of the homepages.

# 9 Conclusion and Future Research Directions

## Introduction

As has been demonstrated throughout this book, the topic of digital multimodal composing (DMC) has piqued the interest of scholars in multiple fields. Despite its relative infancy, DMC has already become a robust topic of inquiry among those teachers and researchers who work in applied linguistics, education and related subfields such as computer-assisted language learning (CALL), educational technology and second language (L2) writing. In this book, I set out to synthesize some of the chief contributions to the topic of DMC, and specifically, to highlight studies and other works that have the capacity to speak to different facets of the second language acquisition (SLA) process. This included discussing the key theories and concepts that have motivated researchers' work (Chapter 2); scholarship that has investigated L2 learners' composing processes when engaging in DMC tasks (Chapter 3); research examining outcomes and evidence of L2 learning (Chapter 4); teachers' and students' perceptions of engaging with different DMC activities (Chapter 5); and the influence of DMC tasks on individual differences (IDs) such as identity, motivation and metacognition (Chapter 6). In addition to these thematic research-focused chapters, I also discussed some of the more practical classroom-oriented aspects of DMC, including the different types of tasks and activities that are available to teachers (in Chapter 7), and finally, how teachers might assess learners' DMC products and processes in their local classroom contexts (Chapter 8).

Clearly, the body of research contained within this book strongly suggests that, if used appropriately, DMC tasks have the capacity to positively influence numerous facets of SLA. Thus, despite some initial skepticism by L2 writing scholars (e.g. Manchón, 2017; Qu, 2017), the evidence on DMC now shows that students generally find DMC tasks to be motivating and enjoyable; that such tasks offer L2 learners different means of communicating and expressing their identities; and perhaps most importantly (from a teacher's perspective), that DMC tasks can promote the development of various skills, including students' writing and oral speech. However, as mentioned, DMC itself is still a relatively new topic. This is especially true as far as the social sciences are concerned, with most of the research on DMC having been conducted during the past 10–15 years (see Lim and Kessler [2023] for a research timeline). Because of this, there is still ample room to build upon the foundations of existing work. There is also room to fill in gaps that currently exist in the literature.

This final chapter is devoted to discussing some of these future research directions. In particular, based on the content chapters in the book (i.e. Chapters 2–8), this chapter expounds on some of those major needs that were identified, with an eye toward connecting theory, research and practice with DMC. In the next section, several future research directions are proposed, which are referred to as 'research tasks'. These research tasks are meant to serve as a starting point for graduate students, faculty and teachers who may be interested in conducting DMC-focused research in a range of instructional contexts. When proposing future research tasks, justifications are provided as to why each topic is worthy of further investigation, including sample suggestions for how such studies might be conducted. Finally, after discussing future research directions, in the last section of this chapter, I provide some brief concluding remarks to summarize the major points that were covered in the book.

## Future Research Directions

> Research task #1: Investigate DMC's influence by adopting a specific theory of SLA, education or general human learning/development

The first research task emerges from Chapter 2, which focused on discussing the key theories and concepts that have motivated researchers' investigations of DMC thus far. In that chapter, multiple theories derived from a range of fields such as education, psychology and SLA were reviewed. In total, seven theories were discussed including: systemic functional linguistics (SFL) (Halliday, 1978, 1985), social semiotics (e.g. Hodge & Kress, 1988; Jewitt & Kress, 2003), multiliteracies (New London Group, 1996), interactionist approaches (e.g. Long, 1996; Schmidt, 1990; Swain, 1985), sociocultural theory (Vygotsky, 1978), activity theory (Engeström, 1987; Leont'ev, 1978) and metacognition theory (Flavell, 1979).

It is important to note here that, although DMC scholars have often drawn upon these theories to motivate their work, a large number of published studies appear to lack clear theoretical grounding. That is, sometimes the authors of DMC studies have referred to multimodality rather vaguely in their work, simply citing previous studies in the area of multimodal composing rather than explicitly mentioning a specific theory or theoretical construct in order to situate their research. To put it bluntly: this is problematic. This is because when authors engage in this practice, their studies become very difficult to interpret. I say this because multimodality in itself is *not* a theory. It is a term that refers to specific, observable phenomena involving how two or more modes operate (or are used by people) in a given context. I will not call out specific studies by name here that have engaged in this practice; however, when researchers simply situate their work by saying that they will *investigate multimodality*, or *examine the effects of multimodality*, or something similar without ever mentioning a guiding theory or framework, it is difficult for readers to confidently draw conclusions from the findings of their studies, particularly so when it comes to understanding the nature of SLA (see Chapter 2 for a thorough discussion).

Therefore, future researchers need to carefully attend to this issue by clearly grounding their work in a specific theory of SLA, education or in a theory of general human learning/development. Traditionally, researchers who have been interested in DMC have often drawn upon multiliteracies (New London Group, 1996) and/or SFL (Halliday, 1978, 1985). Future researchers might also consider drawing on one of these prominent theories. However, depending on one's own theoretical positioning and personal research agenda, researchers might also consider drawing on another existing (or even a novel) theory to motivate their work. As discussed in Chapter 2, a multitude of theories must be adopted for the purposes of investigating and interrogating DMC's use in a number of instructional contexts. Adopting a theory enables quantitative and mixed methods researchers to test different hypotheses and to make predictions about the nature of SLA. Similarly, for researchers who adopt qualitative methods, different theoretical lenses enable them to better understand the complex nature of individuals' behaviors.

As such, future studies are welcomed that attempt to adopt any of those lesser explored theories that were mentioned in this book, namely: interactionist approaches, sociocultural theory, activity theory and metacognition theory. Studies are also welcomed that are grounded in other theories that have not been investigated in conjunction with DMC, including (but not limited to) usage-based approaches (see Ellis & Wulff, 2020) and complex dynamic systems theory (see Larsen-Freeman, 2020). For a comprehensive discussion of theories in SLA, readers are encouraged to see VanPatten *et al.* (2020).

Research task #2: Examine DMC's impact on L2 learners of target languages other than English, including in second and/or foreign language contexts

The next research task stems from a review of the research-oriented chapters in this book (i.e. Chapters 3–6). In particular, this task pertains to expanding the target language (TL) and focal populations involved in DMC studies by investigating DMC's use and impact on learners of languages *other* than English. This is a pressing need that has been discussed in a small number of recent publications (e.g. Li, 2022; Lim & Kessler, 2022). Specifically, consumers of both this book and other published DMC studies more broadly will note that when it comes to investigating DMC, researchers have overwhelmingly tended to focus on studying L2 English learners as the primary focal population. Illustrative of this issue is a review study conducted by Zhang *et al.* (2023). In their article, the authors reviewed 60 DMC studies published between 2005 and 2020, and they noted that 93.3% of all the studies they reviewed ($k = 56$) focused on students who were learning English as the TL. It is true that several studies have included non-TL English populations in their designs (e.g. Nishioka, 2016; Vandommele *et al.*, 2017). However, for the most part, it seems that to date, we as researchers can only claim to have a relatively solid grasp of DMC's effects on the learning of English as an additional language.

Expanding the TL of focus is particularly important because numerous theories of multimodal communication (e.g. social semiotics) and of general human learning/development (e.g. sociocultural theory) posit that communication, language and even mode use are largely cultural constructs, which in turn, may be socially and culturally dependent in terms of their use. Therefore, research is needed that includes L2 learner populations beyond that of English. Research is also needed with such languages in second and foreign language contexts.

For example, for those researchers who are primarily interested in conducting quantitative or mixed methods work, studies are welcomed that attempt to replicate existing DMC studies with TLs other than English (see Porte and McManus [2018] for a broader discussion of replication research in applied linguistics). Additionally, for all types of methodological approaches (i.e. quantitative, qualitative and mixed methods), future studies are needed that attempt to facilitate direct comparisons between DMC's use in the learning of different languages. This could be accomplished through a comparative study with L2 learners in the same context (e.g. in a foreign language classroom at a university) but with students who are learning different TLs in two different classes (e.g. in a French course versus in a Chinese course). This could also be accomplished by comparing learners of the same TL (e.g. Korean), but who are learning in different instructional contexts (e.g. in Korea versus in the United States). In general, because there are so few studies examining DMC in conjunction with languages other than English, future studies are welcomed that investigate any of those topics discussed in this book.

Research task #3: Explore the longitudinal effects of DMC on various dimensions of L2 learning

Similar to the second research task, the third research task stems from a review of all four research-focused chapters in this book, and it pertains to the duration of studies' designs. In particular, more longitudinal research exploring the use of DMC is needed. Admittedly, defining what constitutes 'longitudinal' is quite challenging, since some researchers may have different definitions depending on the specific topic and the type of research that they are conducting (see Ortega and Iberri-Shea [2005] for a discussion). Yet, very few studies to date have looked at the long-term effects of DMC, particularly beyond that of one academic semester (i.e. approximately 15–16 weeks). One notable exception is Lee (2014). In Chapter 4, Lee's case study of two English as a foreign language (EFL) writers was discussed, in which Lee examined the repeated effects of various DMC tasks by collecting data over two years, including data that consisted of students' DMC projects, their discussion board postings and surveys. However, this type of longitudinal design is extremely rare among the published literature, as most studies have tended to last only a few weeks or the duration of one academic semester.

Of course, this is somewhat understandable. For one, since DMC activities have only started to gain attention during the past decade, it has likely been challenging for researchers and teachers to make large changes to existing curricula, especially prior to there being some kind of evidence of DMC's effectiveness for SLA purposes. Second, as multiple scholars have noted, conducting longitudinal research is inherently challenging, in that doing so not only takes time, but often also requires funding to sustain the project and continued access to the participant pool (with a risk of attrition the longer the study continues). For qualitative studies, too, there are additional challenges, such as determining how to handle and analyze large amounts of data, which can be labor intensive (Maloney & Kessler, 2019).

However, in order to move the field forward, studies are now needed which attempt to understand the various effects of DMC beyond that of one academic semester. Similar to research task #2, this pertains to all of those areas discussed in this book, including studies that explore how L2 learners' DMC composing processes may vary or evolve over time; the longitudinal effects of DMC tasks and pedagogies on a myriad of L2 learning outcomes (e.g. reading, writing, speaking and listening skills, in addition to pragmatic skills); the extent to which teachers' and students' perceptions of DMC tasks and curricula may change over time; and the long-term effects of DMC tasks and pedagogies on IDs such as identity, motivation and metacognition (see research task #6 for a discussion of IDs).

> Research task #4: Expand the focus of researching DMC's effects to include additional targets and skill areas

In Chapter 4, the topic of DMC's influence on various outcomes and evidence of learning was explored. In that chapter, primary emphasis was given to discussing those studies that operationalized L2 learning outcomes and development in terms of oral and/or written linguistic modes. This decision was made primarily for two reasons: (1) DMC's influence on additional areas such as IDs was given its own chapter (i.e. Chapter 7) and (2) most researchers who have investigated DMC's impact have tended to focus on the written linguistic mode (and only occasionally on oral production). Of course, this also makes a lot of sense because L2 writing researchers are typically keenly interested in understanding DMC's affordances and drawbacks for L2 writing instructional purposes. In the literature to date, most researchers have investigated the influence of DMC by operationalizing L2 writing development in a myriad of ways. This includes investigating DMC's effects on students' written output in the form of different syntactic complexity and/or accuracy measures (e.g. Kim & Belcher, 2020; Vandommele *et al.*, 2017; Xu, 2021); by analyzing the content and organization of students' writing (e.g. Cho & Kim, 2021); and by investigating students' revision behaviors (e.g. Dzekoe, 2017), among other foci.

In addition to focusing on the written linguistic mode, Chapter 4 also highlighted a select number of studies that investigated DMC's influence on other areas related to L2 development. For instance, Tseng (2021) looked at the impact of DMC tasks on students' genre knowledge. Additionally, Yang *et al.* (2020) examined DMC's ability to influence other skill areas, such as students' L2 oral production and their creative thinking capabilities. Investigating the effects of DMC on L2 writing skills is still an area with considerable room for innovation and exploration. However, future research agendas should also be expanded to examine the effects of DMC on other skills such as reading, speaking and listening, along with the aforementioned areas and more (e.g. genre knowledge, creative thinking). This is important because DMC tasks and activities are inherently multimodal, meaning that they typically involve multiple modes, and thus, multiple skills in practice.

In terms of how such studies might be conducted, quasi-experimental designs are greatly needed. One example of a quasi-experimental design that researchers might consider adopting is to recruit an instructor (or to personally serve as the instructor) and to teach two different courses. The first course would adopt a more traditional manner and approach to L2 writing instruction by teaching monomodal essays (e.g. argumentative essays, compare and contrast, summary and response); however, the second course would adopt a series of one specific DMC task type in place of the monomodal essays (e.g. digital video projects or digital posters). This type of design could adopt a pretest and a posttest to assess students' development. Or, if occurring in a class with absolute beginners, the design might consist of a posttest only. Regardless, the test itself should attempt to assess multiple areas of L2 development such as students' reading, writing, speaking, listening and grammatical competence, rather than examining one target only. This type of design could provide considerable insights into the extent to which DMC tasks compare to monomodal writing instruction, particularly when developing L2 learners' skills in a range of areas.

Research task #5: Examine the differential effects of various DMC tasks on L2 learning outcomes and individual differences

The fifth research task emerges from two different chapters in the book: Chapter 4 (on the topic of outcomes and evidence of learning) and Chapter 7 (on the topic of DMC tasks and activities). In Chapter 7, the different types of DMC tasks and activities that have been utilized by researchers in their studies were systematically reviewed. This review consisted of analyzing all those studies discussed in this book in addition to analyzing those DMC studies published more broadly with designs that have investigated some aspect of SLA. In total, 68 studies were reviewed and 14 different types of DMC tasks and activities were found to have been used. This list included DMC tasks such as digital storytelling (used in 33.8% of all studies), digital videos (32.4%), slideshow presentations (10.3%), digital posters (5.9%), research proposals or essays (5.9%), blogs or websites (5.9%) and several more task types (see Chapter 7 for the complete listing). What is important to note here is that although some of these tasks share similarities, there are also clear differences among them. That is, each of these tasks requires different types of skills on the part of the learner (e.g. the ability to effectively leverage different digital tools). These tasks may also require learners to manipulate a range of different modes for the purpose of conveying intended meanings.

Therefore, one currently unexplored (and rather general) question is: Are specific DMC tasks more effective in influencing the development of certain L2 skills? Relatedly, are specific tasks better or more effective in terms of impacting IDs? In this vein, future studies are needed that attempt to examine the differential nature of DMC tasks and activities. In the published literature thus far, most researchers have typically investigated one type of DMC task in their studies, or conversely, they have integrated multiple types of DMC activities into a broader curriculum in an attempt to understand DMC's general influence. For example, in Tseng's (2021) study, the researcher examined a combination of slideshow presentations, digital posters and digital videos. However, differences among these tasks were not explored. Thus, studies are now needed that attempt to compare the relative effects of different DMC tasks.

In terms of how future studies might address this research task, concerning qualitative methods, researchers might consider adopting a case study design or a classroom-based ethnographic approach. When doing so, researchers could follow either one or a small number of L2 learners as they engage with different types of DMC tasks over the span of an academic semester (or a longer period of time, see research task #3). When doing so, researchers could investigate students' perceptions of the different tasks that they engage in, including students' beliefs about their relative effectiveness in promoting their L2 reading, writing, speaking and listening skills, among other target areas. Relatedly, qualitative researchers might also investigate IDs such as motivation and identity, and correspondingly, the extent to which the focal ID is impacted by the use of different types of DMC tasks.

In terms of studies leveraging quantitative or mixed methods, similar to the previous research task, quasi-experimental designs are needed. For example, a quasi-experimental design could be adopted with two different course sections, in which the first section implements a series of one specific DMC task type during the semester (e.g. digital video projects), while the second section adopts a different type of DMC task (e.g. digital posters). Once again, such a design might utilize a pretest and a posttest, or a posttest only if occurring with absolute beginners of the TL. This type of design would likely provide interesting information about the extent to which two DMC task types are effective for the purposes of advancing specific L2 skills, or in terms of influencing IDs.

> Research task #6: Expand the scope of individual differences research to include IDs beyond motivation and identity

The topic of IDs was covered in Chapter 6. In that chapter, the focus was on describing a number of DMC studies that have examined one of three IDs, including identity, motivation and metacognition. These three IDs were selected as the primary targets, in large part, because a majority of the existing research has tended to focus on them, and more specifically, on the two IDs of identity and motivation. Although there is a sizable body of work on both identity and motivation, as discussed earlier, future research is still needed that examines these IDs with learners of languages other than English (see research task #2). Research is also needed that investigates the differential effects of DMC tasks and activities on these IDs (see research task #5). In addition to these tasks, scholarship is also needed that broadens the scope of ID research to focus on DMC's impact on other IDs that have received little to no attention thus far.

For example, although metacognition was discussed in Chapter 6, there are very few studies in this area. Because of this, future studies investigating DMC's impact on aspects of L2 learners' metacognition are strongly encouraged. In addition to metacognition, a number of other IDs are worthy of investigation. These include (but are not limited to) students' learning styles and strategies (see Griffiths, 2022), willingness to communicate (see Peng, 2022) and anxiety (see MacIntyre & Wang, 2022). Future researchers might look to those previous studies discussed in Chapter 6 as a means of formulating their research designs. As noted, most of the scholarship involving DMC and IDs has been qualitative in scope. Such research has primarily been accomplished through adopting case study designs and by following a select number of L2 learners as they engage in one or more DMC tasks. Therefore, future studies are needed that adopt quantitative or mixed methods designs for operationalizing and measuring IDs.

Another potentially interesting ID to examine, which has not been extensively researched thus far, is that of learners' ages. For instance, DMC-oriented studies have traditionally looked at a single age or learner group only (i.e. one classroom of children in a K-12 context or one classroom of adults in a university context). Because much DMC scholarship has investigated L2 learners' composing processes, it would therefore be interesting to understand the extent to which different age groups approach, interact with and compose the same type of DMC task (e.g. a digital poster or a storyboarding activity). That is, to what extent do younger children, adolescents and adults engage in the same task similarly and/or differently? How do these different age groups orchestrate and leverage modes in order to create intended meanings? And, what might these observations and findings tell us about the nexus of age, SLA and how learners attempt to communicate via multiple modes? (For a general discussion of age and SLA, see Singleton and Pfenninger [2022].)

Clearly, there is still much room to expand future research agendas for the purposes of studying the intersection of DMC and IDs. Those readers who are interested in learning more about the IDs discussed in this section and more are encouraged to see Li et al.'s (2022a) comprehensive handbook, which covers research methods involving IDs in the domain of SLA.

> Research task #7: Investigate and experiment with the use of product-based and process-based assessment for grading various DMC tasks and activities

The seventh and final research task comes from Chapter 8, which examined the topic of DMC assessment. In the chapter, assessment was discussed in a very practical sense, particularly in terms of how L2 writing teachers and other educators might assess students' DMC projects using either a product-based or a process-based approach. The topic of assessment is particularly important (for a number of obvious reasons), yet more so because it currently constitutes a major hurdle to many teachers implementing DMC in their own classrooms. Whereas teachers often receive considerable training on assessing L2 learners' linguistic skills in their educational programs, they rarely (if ever) receive explicit instruction regarding the assessment of non-linguistic modes.

When reviewing product-based assessment studies (i.e. studies that examine only the final DMC project produced by students), a number of articles were described in detail, in which the authors conducted action research to explore the use of different types of grading rubrics. For example, in Hung *et al.* (2013), the authors examined a rubric that was created for grading slideshow presentations; Ørevik (2022) examined a rubric for assessing digital posters; and finally, Jiang *et al.* (2022) examined a genre-based rubric, which they suggested could potentially be used for assessing a variety of DMC task types (e.g. digital videos and digital posters). As discussed in Chapter 8, the topic of DMC assessment has been underexplored in general, especially when compared to other topics that are addressed in this book. Therefore, future studies are needed that further examine the use of these rubrics described in Hung *et al.* (2013), Ørevik (2022) and Jiang *et al.* (2022). Specifically, future researchers might examine the perceived utility of these rubrics from teachers' perspectives in different instructional contexts. Jiang *et al.*'s rubric needs to be investigated when used with a variety of multimodal genres. In addition to examining these rubrics from the perspective of teachers, future studies might also explore the extent to which raters can achieve inter-rater reliability when using these rubrics. That is, how consistently can raters assess students' DMC projects using these rubrics and when assessing non-linguistic modes?

In turning from product-based to process-based assessment (i.e. grading students' work at multiple stages throughout the act of composing, rather than at only one point in time), one key study by Hafner and Ho (2020) was discussed. In their study, Hafner and Ho advocated for expanding DMC assessment practices to occur during four main stages: (1) pre-design, (2) design, (3) sharing and (4) reflecting. However, apart from Hafner and Ho's study, very little is known about the implementation of process-based assessment practices with DMC. For example, in different contexts, to what extent do teachers find these four stages practical, easy to implement and easy to grade? Can this process-based model be implemented in small-, medium- and large-sized classes alike? What successes and challenges do teachers face when attempting to implement it? Finally, to what extent does a process-based model of assessment impact student learning outcomes when compared to a product-based model of assessment?

As is evident, there is still a considerable amount of room for future studies to explore issues of DMC assessment, as relatively little has been done in this area. Future research agendas should expand and attempt to tackle the aforementioned issues head-on, including those involving product-based and/or process-based assessment with DMC. To learn more about language assessment, readers are encouraged to see Winke and Brunfaut's (2021) comprehensive handbook.

## Concluding Remarks

The primary goal of this book has been to provide graduate students, teachers, researchers and faculty with an introduction to and overview of the topic of DMC, particularly as it pertains to the teaching and learning of second or additional languages. As highlighted throughout the book, DMC is both an emerging and flourishing area of scholarly inquiry, which has captured the attention of researchers and practitioners from a number of academic disciplines. Much of the work that has been conducted thus far – especially at the intersection of DMC and SLA – has been highly interdisciplinary in nature. To understand the effects and influence of DMC tasks on aspects related to L2 learning, researchers have drawn on both cognitive and sociocultural-oriented theories from a number of fields and have also adopted a number of diverse methods and tools for investigating various phenomena. Due to the fast-paced, ever-changing and increasingly accessible nature of digital technologies, it seems that the potential for innovative research with DMC is endless, and it is likely that the number of studies will continue to grow exponentially in the coming years. Thus, although I hope that readers will strongly consider the research tasks outlined in this chapter as a starting point, I also hope that readers will venture far beyond these suggestions and investigate any/all lines of inquiry that may emerge over time.

In moving from theory and research to the issue of pedagogy, there is also a considerable amount of work to be done. As I have attempted to stress throughout this book, the links between theory, research and pedagogy are symbiotic, feeding into each other rather than being a rigid or established hierarchy. Therefore, because a sizable amount of research and theory often emerge from specific observations that occur within a classroom setting, I strongly encourage language teachers to experiment with some of the DMC tasks and activities that have been discussed throughout the book. The work that teachers do, in this regard, is incredibly important. Teacher-initiated action research studies are needed in order to investigate a variety of DMC tasks across diverse instructional contexts, including experimenting with such tasks when teaching different TLs, age groups, class sizes and more.

Another important note is that a large portion of CALL research that is published in academic journals and book chapters often focuses heavily on success stories only. That is, when specific types of DMC tasks and activities work well, teachers and researchers are more inclined to report them. However, we, as a community, also need to gain a thorough understanding of when and in what situations DMC may not work (along with *why* it may not work). Thus, in the future, teachers and researchers are encouraged to report any and all findings, including those that may shine a positive and/or negative light on the pedagogical applications of DMC in a given context. Only by understanding the full scope and effects of DMC in a range of varied contexts can we understand how to use (or how not to use) different DMC tasks appropriately for the purposes of fostering SLA.

In closing, I hope that this book serves as a useful guide for those readers who are interested in issues pertaining to SLA theory, research and pedagogy with DMC. This topic area is one that clearly has tremendous potential, in terms of what has already been discovered and in terms of the frontier that lies ahead.

# References

Abdel-Hack, E.M. and Helwa, H.S.A.-H.A. (2014) Using digital storytelling and weblogs instruction to enhance EFL narrative writing and critical thinking skills among EFL majors at faculty of education. *Educational Research* 5 (1), 8–41.

Accurso, K. and Walsh Marr, J.M. (2024) Systemic functional linguistics and the (expanded) teaching and learning cycle. In M. Kessler and C. Polio (eds) *Conducting Genre-Based Research in Applied Linguistics: A Methodological Guide* (pp. 221–244). Routledge.

Ahmadian, M.J., Mansouri, S.A. and Ghominejad, S. (2017) Language learners' and teachers' perceptions of task repetition. *ELT Journal* 71, 467–477. https://doi.org/10.1093/elt/ccx011

Ajayi, L. (2011) How ESL teachers' sociocultural identities mediate their teacher role identities in a diverse urban school setting. *The Urban Review* 43, 654–680. https://doi.org/10.1007/s11256-010-0161-y

Akoto, M. (2021) Collaborative multimodal writing via Google Docs: Perceptions of French FL learners. *Languages* 6 (3). https://doi.org/10.3390/languages6030140

Aljaafreh, A. and Lantolf, J.P. (1994) Negative feedback as regulation and second language learning in the Zone of Proximal Development. *The Modern Language Journal* 78 (4), 465–483. https://doi.org/10.1111/j.1540-4781.1994.tb02064.x

Alrabai, F. (2022) The predictive role of anxiety and motivation in L2 proficiency: An empirical causal model. *Language Teaching Research*. https://doi.org/10.1177/13621688221136247

Andiliou, A. and Murphy, P.K. (2010) Examining variations among researchers' and teachers' conceptualizations of creativity: A review and synthesis of contemporary research. *Educational Research Review* 5 (3), 201–219. https://doi.org/10.1016/j.edurev.2010.07.003

Applebee, A.N. (1986) Problems in process approaches: Toward a reconceptualization of process instruction. In A. Petrosky and D. Bartholomae (eds) *The Teaching of Writing* (pp. 95–113). University of Chicago Press.

Azis, Y.A. and Mataram, H. (2020) Collaborative digital storytelling-based task for EFL writing instruction: Outcomes and perceptions. *Journal of Asia TEFL* 17 (2), 562–579. http://dx.doi.org/10.18823/asiatefl.2020.17.2.16.562

Balaman, S. (2018) Digital storytelling: A multimodal narrative writing genre. *Journal of Language and Linguistic Studies* 14 (3), 202–212.

Bateman, J. (2008) *Multimodality and Genre: A Foundation for the Systematic Analysis of Multimodal Documents*. Palgrave Macmillan.

Biber, D., Gray, B. and Poonpon, K. (2011) Should we use characteristics of conversation to measure grammatical complexity in L2 writing development? *TESOL Quarterly* 45 (1), 5–35. https://doi.org/10.5054/tq.2011.244483

Bikowski, D. and Vithanage, R. (2016) Effects of web-based collaborative writing on individual L2 writing development. *Language Learning & Technology* 20 (1), 79–99. http://llt.msu.edu/issues/february2016/bikowskivithanage.pdf

Block, D. (2007) The rise of identity in SLA research, post Firth and Wagner (1997). *The Modern Language Journal* 91 (1), 863–876. https://doi.org/10.1111/j.1540-4781.2007.00674.x

Block, D. (2013) Moving beyond 'lingualism': Multilingual embodiment and multimodality in SLA. In S. May (ed.) *The Multilingual Turn: Implications for SLA, TESOL, and Bilingual Education* (pp. 54–77). Routledge.

Bowles, M.A. (2019) Verbal reports in instructed SLA research: Opportunities, challenges, and limitations. In R.P. Leow (ed.) *The Routledge Handbook of Second Language Research in Classroom Learning* (pp. 31–43). Routledge.

Boyne, J. (2019) *My Brother's Name is Jessica*. Penguin.

Brown, A.L. (1978) Knowing when, where, and how to remember: A problem of metacognition. In R. Glaser (ed.) *Advances in Instructional Psychology* (pp. 77–165). Erlbaum.

Brown, H.D. and Lee, H. (2015) *Teaching by Principles: An Interactive Approach to Language Pedagogy* (4th edn). Pearson.

Buck, P.S. (1976) *The Big Wave*. Harper Trophy.

Bui, G. and Kong, A. (2019) Metacognitive instruction for peer review interaction in L2 writing. *Journal of Writing Research* 11 (2), 357–392. https://doi.org/10.17239/jowr-2019.11.02.05

Campbell, E. and Storch, N. (2011) The changing face of motivation: A study of second language learners' motivation over time. *Australian Review of Applied Linguistics* 34 (2), 166–192. https://doi.org/10.1075/aral.34.2.03cam

Campoy-Cubillo, M.C. and Querol-Julián, M. (2022) Assessing multimodal listening comprehension through online informative videos: The operationalisation of a new listening framework for ESP in higher education. In S. Diamantopoulou and S. Ørevik (eds) *Multimodality in English Language Learning* (pp. 228–256). Routledge.

Canale, G. (2022) Designing for assessment as recognition of multimodal work in the EAL classroom. In S. Diamantopoulou and S. Ørevik (eds) *Multimodality in English Language Learning* (pp. 207–220). Routledge.

Carless, D. (2007) The suitability of task-based approaches for secondary schools: Perspectives from Hong Kong. *System* 35, 595–608. https://doi.org/10.1016/j.system.2007.09.003

Castañeda, M.E. (2013) 'I am proud that I did it and it's a piece of me': Digital storytelling in the foreign language classroom. *CALICO Journal* 30 (1), 44–62. https://www.jstor.org/stable/calicojournal.30.1.44

Castañeda, M.E., Shen, X. and Claros Berlioz, E.M. (2018) This is my story: Latinx learners create digital stories during a summer literacy camp. *TESOL Journal* 9 (4), 1–14. https://doi.org/10.1002/tesj.378

Charmaz, K. (2014) *Constructing Grounded Theory*. Sage.

Chen, C.W.Y. (2018) Developing EFL students' digital empathy through video production. *System* 77, 50–57. https://doi.org/10.1016/j.system.2018.01.006

Chen, Q. and Wright, C. (2017) Contextualization and authenticity in TBLT: Voices from Chinese classrooms. *Language Teaching Research* 21, 517–538. https://doi.org/10.1177/1362168816639985

Cho, H. and Kim, Y. (2021) Comparing the characteristics of EFL students' multimodal composing and traditional monomodal writing: The case of a reading-to-write task. *Language Teaching Research*, 1–26. https://doi.org/10.1177/13621688211046740

Cimasko, T. and Shin, D. (2017) Multimodal resemiotization and authorial agency in an L2 writing classroom. *Written Communication* 34 (4), 387–413. https://doi.org/10.1177/0741088317727246

Cole, D.R. and Pullen, D.L. (eds) (2010) *Multiliteracies in Motion: Current Theory and Practice*. Routledge.

Cope, B. and Kalantzis, M. (2009) 'Multiliteracies': New literacies, new meaning. *Pedagogies: An International Journal* 4 (3), 164–195. https://doi.org/10.1080/15544800903076044

Coulthard, M., Johnson, A. and Wright, D. (2017) *An Introduction to Forensic Linguistics: Language in Evidence* (2nd edn). Routledge.

Cowie, N. (2018) Student transcription for reflective language learning. *ELT Journal* 72 (4), 435–444. https://doi.org/10.1093/elt/ccy010

Csizér, K. (2019) The L2 motivational self system. In M. Lamb, K. Csizér, A. Henry and S. Ryan (eds) *The Palgrave Handbook of Motivation for Language Learning* (pp. 71–93). Palgrave Macmillan.

D'Angelo, L. and Marino, F. (2024) Multimodal analysis. In M. Kessler and C. Polio (eds) *Conducting Genre-Based Research in Applied Linguistics: A Methodological Guide* (pp. 172–198). Routledge.

Dahlström, H. (2022) Students as digital multimodal text designers: A study of resources, affordances, and experiences. *British Journal of Educational Technology* 53 (2), 391–407. https://doi.org/10.1111/bjet.13171

Dávila, L.T. and Susberry, V. (2021) Multimodal and multilingual co-authoring in high school social studies ESL classrooms. In D.-S. Shin, T. Cimasko and Y. Yi (eds) *Multimodal Composing in K-16 ESL and EFL Education* (pp. 55–71). Springer.

De Costa, P.I. and Norton, B. (2016) Identity in language learning and teaching. In S. Preece (ed.) *The Routledge Handbook of Language and Identity* (pp. 586–601). Routledge.

De Costa, P.I., Kessler, M. and Gajasinghe, K. (2022) Ethnography. In S. Li, P. Hiver and M. Papi (eds) *The Routledge Handbook of Second Language Acquisition and Individual Differences* (pp. 427–440). Routledge.

de Jager, A., Fogarty, A., Tewson, A., Lenette, C. and Boydell, K.M. (2017) Digital storytelling in research: A systematic review. *The Qualitative Report* 22 (10), 2548–2582. https://doi.org/10.46743/2160-3715/2017.2970

Dewaele, J., Witney, J., Saito, K. and Dewaele, L. (2017) Foreign language enjoyment and anxiety: The effect of teacher and learner variables. *Language Teaching Research* 22 (6), 676–697. https://doi.org/10.1177/1362168817692161

Donato, R. (1994) Collective scaffolding in second language learning. In J.P. Lantolf and G. Appel (eds) *Vygotskian Approaches to Second Language Research* (pp. 33–56). Ablex.

Donker, A., de Boer, H., Kostons, D., van Ewijk, C.D. and van der Werf, M. (2014) Effectiveness of learning strategy instruction on academic performance: A meta-analysis. *Educational Research Review* 11, 1–26. https://doi.org/10.1016/j.edurev.2013.11.002

Dörnyei, Z. (1994) Understanding L2 motivation: On with the challenge! *The Modern Language Journal* 78 (4), 515–523. https://doi.org/10.2307/328590

Dörnyei, Z. (2009) The L2 motivational self system. In Z. Dörnyei and E. Ushioda (eds) *Motivation, Language Identity and the L2 Self* (pp. 9–42). Multilingual Matters.

Duff, P.A. (2008) *Case Study Research in Applied Linguistics*. Routledge.

Dzekoe, R. (2017) Computer-based multimodal composing activities, self-revision, and L2 acquisition through writing. *Language Learning & Technology* 21 (2), 73–95. http://llt.msu.edu/issues/june2017/dzekoe.pdf

Ellis, N.C. and Wulff, S. (2020) Usage-based approaches to L2 acquisition. In B. VanPatten, G.D. Keating and S. Wulff (eds) *Theories in Second Language Acquisition* (3rd edn, pp. 63–82). Routledge.

Ellis, R. (2004) Individual differences in second language learning. In A. Davies and C. Elder (eds) *The Handbook of Applied Linguistics* (pp. 525–551). Wiley-Blackwell.

Ellis, R. (2017) Task-based language teaching. In S. Loewen and M. Sato (eds) *The Routledge Handbook of Instructed Second Language Acquisition* (pp. 108–125). Routledge.

Ellis, R. (2022) Foreword. In S. Li, P. Hiver and M. Papi (eds) *The Routledge Handbook of Second Language Acquisition and Individual Differences* (pp. xxiv–xxvii). Routledge.

Ellis, R. and Shintani, N. (2014) *Exploring Language Pedagogy through Second Language Acquisition Research*. Routledge.

Engeström, Y. (1987) *Learning by Expanding: An Activity Theoretical Approach to Developmental Research*. Orienta-Konsultit Oy.

Engeström, Y. (1999) Activity theory and individual and social transformation. In Y. Engeström, R. Miettinen and R.-L. Punamäki (eds) *Perspective on Activity Theory: Learning in Doing: Social, Cognitive and Computational Perspectives* (pp. 19–38). Cambridge.

Engin, M. (2014) Extending the flipped classroom model: Developing second language writing skills through student-created digital videos. *Journal of the Scholarship of Teaching and Learning* 14 (5), 12–26. https://doi.org/10.14434/12829

Farrell, T.S.C. (2011) Exploring the professional role identities of novice ESL teachers through reflective practice. *System* 39 (1), 54–62. https://doi.org/10.1016/j.system.2011.01.012

Fidalgo, P., Thormann, J., Kulyk, O. and Lencastre, J.A. (2020) Students' perceptions on distance education: A multinational study. *International Journal of Educational Technology in Higher Education* 17 (18). https://doi.org/10.1186/s41239-020-00194-2

Flavell, J.H. (1979) Metacognition and cognitive monitoring: A new area of cognitive–developmental inquiry. *American Psychologist* 34 (10), 906–911. https://doi.org/10.1037/0003-066X.34.10.906

Gao, J., Pham, Q.H.P. and Polio, C. (2022) The role of theory in quantitative and qualitative second language learning research: A corpus-based analysis. *Research Methods in Applied Linguistics* 1 (2), 100006. https://doi.org/10.1016/j.rmal.2022.100006

Gardner, R.C. and Smythe, P.C. (1975) Motivation and second language acquisition. *The Canadian Modern Language Review* 31 (3), 218–233. https://doi.org/10.3138/cmlr.31.3.218

Gardner, R.C. and MacIntyre, R.C. (1991) An instrumental motivation in language study: Who says it isn't effective? *Studies in Second Language Acquisition* 13 (1), 57–72. https://doi.org/10.1017/S0272263100009724

Gass, S.M. and Mackey, A. (2020) Input, interaction, and output in L2 acquisition. In B. VanPatten, G.D. Keating and S. Wulff (eds) *Theories in Second Language Acquisition* (3rd edn, pp. 192–222). Routledge.

Goss, S. (2014) The development of a self-report scale measuring affective, cognitive, and metacognitive dimensions related to study skill and self-regulation skill utilization with middle school students. Unpublished doctoral dissertation, Kent State University.

Griffiths, C. (2022) Learning styles and strategies. In S. Li, P. Hiver and M. Papi (eds) *The Routledge Handbook of Second Language Acquisition and Individual Differences* (pp. 82–94). Routledge.

Guichon, N. and McLornan, S. (2008) The effects of multimodality on L2 learners: Implications for CALL resource design. *System* 36 (1), 85–93. https://doi.org/10.1016/j.system.2007.11.005

Hafner, C.A. (2015) Remix culture and English language teaching: The expression of learner voice in digital multimodal composing. *TESOL Quarterly* 49 (3), 486–509. https://doi.org/10.1002/tesq.238

Hafner, C.A. and Miller, L. (2011) Fostering learner autonomy in English for science: A collaborative digital video project in a technological learning environment. *Language Learning & Technology* 15 (3), 68–86. http://dx.doi.org/10125/44263

Hafner, C.A. and Ho, W.Y.J. (2020) Assessing digital multimodal composing in second language writing: Towards a process-based model. *Journal of Second Language Writing* 47, 100710. https://doi.org/10.1016/j.jslw.2020.100710

Halliday, M.A.K. (1978) *Language as Social Semiotic: The Social Interpretation of Language and Meaning*. Edward Arnold.

Halliday, M.A.K. (1985) *An Introduction to Functional Grammar*. Edward Arnold.

Halliday, M.A.K. and Matthiessen, C.M.I.M. (2004) *An Introduction to Functional Grammar*. Routledge.

Han, Y. (2017) Mediating and being mediated: Learner beliefs and learner engagement with written corrective feedback. *System* 69, 133–142. https://doi.org/10.1016/j.system.2017.07.003

Hava, K. (2021) Exploring the role of digital storytelling in student motivation and satisfaction in EFL education. *Computer Assisted Language Learning* 34 (7), 958–978. https://doi.org/10.1080/09588221.2019.1650071

Henry, A. (2019) Online media creation and L2 motivation: A socially situated perspective. *TESOL Quarterly* 53 (2), 372–404. https://doi.org/10.1002/tesq.485

Hepple, E., Sockhill, M., Tan, A. and Alford, J. (2014) Multiliteracies pedagogy: Creating claymations with adolescent, post-beginner English language learners. *Journal of Adolescent & Adult Literacy* 58 (3), 219–229. https://doi.org/10.1002/jaal.339

Hodge, R. and Kress, G. (1988) *Social Semiotics*. Cornell University Press.

Huang, H.-T.D. (2022) Examining the effect of digital storytelling on English speaking proficiency, willingness to communicate, and group cohesion. *TESOL Quarterly*. https://doi.org/10.1002/tesq.3147

Hung, H.-T., Chiu, Y.-C.J. and Yeh, H.-C. (2013) Multimodal assessment of and for learning: A theory-driven design rubric. *British Journal of Educational Technology* 44 (3), 400–409. https://doi.org/10.1111/j.1467-8535.2012.01337.x

Hung, S.-T.A. (2019) Creating digital stories: EFL learners' engagement, cognitive and metacognitive skills. *Educational Technology & Society* 22 (2), 26–37.

Hyland, K. and Zou, H.J. (2021) 'I believe the findings are fascinating': Stance in three-minute theses. *English for Academic Purposes* 50, 100973. https://doi.org/10.1016/j.jeap.2021.100973

Jewitt, C. (2003) Re-thinking assessment: Multimodality, literacy and computer-mediated learning. *Assessment in Education: Principles, Policy & Practice* 10 (1), 83–102. https://doi.org/10.1080/09695940301698

Jewitt, C. (2006) *Technology, Literacy and Learning: A Multimodal Approach*. Routledge.

Jewitt, C. and Kress, G. (2003) *Multimodal Literacy*. Lang.

Jewitt, C., Bezemer, J. and O'Halloran, K. (2016) *Introducing Multimodality*. Routledge.

Jiang, L. (2017) The affordances of digital multimodal composing for EFL learning. *ELT Journal* 71 (4), 413–422. https://doi.org/10.1093/elt/ccw098

Jiang, L. (2018) Digital multimodal composing and investment change in learners' writing in English as a foreign language. *Journal of Second Language Writing* 40, 60–72. https://doi.org/10.1016/j.jslw.2018.03.002

Jiang, L. and Luk, J. (2016) Multimodal composing as a learning activity in English classrooms: Inquiring into the sources of its motivational capacity. *System* 59, 1–11. https://doi.org/10.1016/j.system.2016.04.001

Jiang, L. and Gao, J. (2020) Fostering EFL learners' digital empathy through multimodal composing. *RELC Journal* 51 (1), 70–85. https://doi.org/10.1177/0033688219898565

Jiang, L. and Ren, W. (2021) Digital multimodal composing in L2 Learning: Ideologies and impact. *Journal of Language, Identity, and Education* 20 (3), 167–182. https://doi.org/10.1080/15348458.2020.1753192

Jiang, L., Yang, M. and Yu, S. (2020) Chinese ethnic minority students' investment in English learning empowered by digital multimodal composing. *TESOL Quarterly* 54 (4), 954–979. https://doi.org/10.1002/tesq.5666

Jiang, L., Yu, S. and Lee, I. (2022) Developing a genre-based model for assessing digital multimodal composing in second language writing: Integrating theory with practice. *Journal of Second Language Writing* 57, 100869. https://doi.org/10.1016/j.jslw.2022.100869

Karimi, M. and Mofidi, M. (2019) L2 teacher identity development: An activity theoretic perspective. *System* 81, 122–134. https://doi.org/10.1016/j.system.2019.02.006

Kessler, G. and Bikowski, D. (2010) Developing collaborative autonomous learning abilities in computer mediated language learning: Attention to meaning among students in wiki space. *Computer Assisted Language Learning* 23 (1), 41–58. https://doi.org/10.1080/09588220903467335

Kessler, G., Bikowski, D. and Boggs, J. (2012) Collaborative writing among second language learners in academic web-based projects. *Language Learning & Technology* 16 (1), 91–109. http://llt.msu.edu/issues/february2012/kesslerbikowskiboggs.pdf

Kessler, M. (2019) Promoting text co-ownership and peer interactions in collaborative writing. *TESOL Journal* 11 (2), e476. https://doi.org/10.1002/tesj.476

Kessler, M. (2020a) Technology-mediated writing: Exploring incoming graduate students' L2 writing strategies with Activity Theory. *Computers and Composition* 55, 102542. https://doi.org/10.1016/j.compcom.2020.102542

Kessler, M. (2020b) Teaching and learning in a content-based classroom: Understanding pedagogy and the development of L2 writers' metacognitive genre awareness. Unpublished doctoral dissertation, Michigan State University.

Kessler, M. (2021a) Investigating connections between teacher identity and pedagogy in a content-based classroom. *System* 100, 102551. https://doi.org/10.1016/j.system.2021.102551

Kessler, M. (2021b) Supplementing mobile-assisted language learning with reflective journal writing: A case study of Duolingo users' metacognitive awareness. *Computer Assisted Language Learning*. https://doi.org/10.1080/09588221.2021.1968914

Kessler, M. (2021c) The longitudinal development of second language writers' metacognitive genre awareness. *Journal of Second Language Writing* 53, 100832. https://doi.org/10.1016/j.jslw.2021.100832

Kessler, M. (2022a) Multimodality. *ELT Journal* 76 (4), 551–554. https://doi.org/10.1093/elt/ccac028

Kessler, M. (2022b) Prospective English language teachers' projected identities in personal statements plus experienced teachers' reactions. *International Journal of Applied Linguistics* 32 (1), 76–93. https://doi.org/10.1111/ijal.12381

Kessler, M. (2023a) Designing collaborative writing tasks for face-to-face and computer-mediated communication contexts. In M. Li and M. Zhang (eds) *L2 Collaborative Writing in Diverse Learning Contexts* (pp. 184–201). John Benjamins.

Kessler, M. (2023b) Written corrective feedback in an online community: A typology of English language learners' requests and interlocutors' responses. *Computers and Composition* 67, 102752. https://doi.org/10.1016/j.compcom.2023.102752

Kessler, M. and Maloney, J. (2019) The use of ethnography in World Englishes. In P.I. De Costa, D. Crowther and J. Maloney (eds) *Investigating World Englishes: Research Methodology and Practical Applications* (pp. 104–121). Routledge.

Kessler, M. and Marino, F. (2023) Digital multimodal composing in English language teaching. *ELT Journal* 77 (3), 370–376. https://doi.org/10.1093/elt/ccac047

Kessler, M. and Polio, C. (eds) (2024a) *Conducting Genre-Based Research in Applied Linguistics: A Methodological Guide*. Routledge.

Kessler, M. and Polio, C. (2024b) Introduction. In M. Kessler and C. Polio (eds) *Conducting Genre-Based Research in Applied Linguistics: A Methodological Guide* (pp. 1–10). Routledge.

Kessler, M., Loewen, S. and Trego, D. (2020a) Synchronous VCMC with TalkAbroad: Exploring noticing, transcription, and learner perceptions in Spanish foreign-language pedagogy. *Language Teaching Research*. https://doi.org/10.1177/1362168820954456

Kessler, M., Solheim, I. and Zhao, M. (2020b) Can task-based language teaching be 'authentic' in foreign language contexts?: Exploring the case of China. *TESOL Journal* 12 (1), e00534. https://doi.org/10.1002/tesj.534

Kim, H. and Lee, J.H. (2017) The value of digital storytelling as an L2 narrative practice. *The Asia-Pacific Education Researcher* 27, 1–9. https://doi.org/10.1007/s40299-017-0360-3

Kim, Y. and Belcher, D. (2020) Multimodal composing and traditional essays: Linguistic performance and learner perceptions. *RELC Journal* 51 (1), 86–100. https://doi.org/10.1177/0033688220906943

Kohnke, L., Jarvis, A. and Ting, A. (2021) Digital multimodal composing as authentic assessment in discipline-specific English courses: Insights from ESP learners. *TESOL Journal* 12 (3), e600. https://doi.org/10.1002/tesj.600

Kormos, J. (2012) The role of individual differences in L2 writing. *Journal of Second Language Writing* 21 (4), 390–403. https://doi.org/10.1016/j.jslw.2012.09.003

Knobel, M. and Lankshear, C. (2008) Remix: The art and craft of endless hybridization. *Journal of Adolescent & Adult Literacy* 52 (1), 22–33. https://doi.org/10.1598/JAAL.52.1.3

Krashen, S. (1981) *Second Language Acquisition and Second Language Learning*. Prentice Hall.

Krashen, S. (1982) *Principles and Practice in Second Language Acquisition*. Prentice Hall.

Kress, G. (2003) *Literacy in the New Media Age*. Routledge.

Kress, G. (2010) *Multimodality: A Social Semiotic Approach to Contemporary Communication*. Routledge.

Kress, G. and van Leeuwen, T. (1996) *Reading Images: The Grammar of Visual Design*. Routledge.

Kress, G. and van Leeuwen, T. (2001) *Multimodal Discourse: The Modes and Media of Contemporary Communication*. Oxford University Press.

Kuiken, F. and Vedder, I. (2017) Functional adequacy in L2 writing: Towards a new rating scale. *Language Testing* 34 (3), 321–336. https://doi.org/10.1177/0265532216663991

Kuiken, F., Vedder, I., Housen, A. and De Clercq, B. (2019) Variation in syntactic complexity: Introduction. *International Journal of Applied Linguistics* 29 (2), 161–170. https://doi.org/10.1111/ijal.12255

Lantolf, J.P., Poehner, M.E. and Thorne, S.L. (2020) Sociocultural theory and L2 development. In B. VanPatten, G.D. Keating and S. Wulff (eds) *Theories in Second Language Acquisition* (3rd edn, pp. 223–247). Routledge.

Larsen-Freeman, D. (2020) Complex dynamic systems theory. In B. VanPatten, G.D. Keating and S. Wulff (eds) *Theories in Second Language Acquisition* (3rd edn, pp. 248–270). Routledge.

Larson-Hall, J. (2016) *A Guide to Doing Statistics in Second Language Research Using SPSS and R* (2nd edn). Routledge.

Lawrence, G. (2014) The role of teachers and their beliefs in implementing technology-mediated language learning: Implications for teacher development and research. *International Journal of Computer-Assisted Language Learning and Teaching* 4 (4). https://doi.org/10.4018/ijcallt.2014100105

Lawrence, G. (2018) The role of language teacher beliefs in an increasingly digitalized world. In B. Zou and M. Thomas (eds) *Handbook of Research on Integrating Technology into Contemporary Language Learning and Teaching* (pp. 140–160). IGI Global.

Lee, B., Chen, Y. and Hewitt, L. (2011) Age differences in constraints encountered by seniors in their use of computers and the internet. *Computers in Human Behavior* 27 (3), 1231–1237. https://doi.org/10.1016/j.chb.2011.01.003

Lee, H.-C. (2014) Using an arts-integrated multimodal approach to promote English learning: A case study of two Taiwanese junior college students. *English Teaching: Practice and Critique* 13 (2), 55–75.

Lee, S., Lo, Y. and Chin, T. (2021) Practicing multiliteracies to enhance EFL learners' meaning making process and language development: A multimodal problem-based approach. *Computer Assisted Language Learning* 34, 66–91. https://doi.org/10.1080/09588221.2019.1614959

Leont'ev, A.N. (1978) *Activity, Consciousness, and Personality*. Prentice Hall.

Leont'ev, A.N. (1981) *Problems of the Development of Mind*. Progress.

Leow, R.P. (2020) L2 writing-to-learn: Theory, research, and a curricular approach. In R.M. Manchón (ed.) *Writing and Language Learning: Advancing Research Agendas* (pp. 95–120). John Benjamins.

Leow, R.P. and Morgan-Short, K. (2004) To think aloud or not to think aloud: Issue of reactivity in SLA research methodology. *Studies in Second Language Acquisition* 26 (1), 35–57. https://doi.org/10.1017/S0272263104026129

Leow, R.P. and Suh, B.-R. (2022) Theoretical perspectives on L2 writing, written corrective feedback, and language learning in individual writing conditions. In R.M. Manchón and C. Polio (eds) *The Routledge Handbook of Second Language Acquisition and Writing* (pp. 9–21). Routledge.

Lessig, L. (2008) *Remix: Making Art and Commerce Thrive in the Hybrid Economy*. Penguin Press.

Li, M. (2020) Multimodal pedagogy in TESOL teacher education: Students' perspectives. *System* 94, 102337. https://doi.org/10.1016/j.system.2020.102337

Li, M. (2022) *Researching and Teaching Second Language Writing in the Digital Age*. Palgrave Macmillan.

Li, M. and Akoto, M. (2021) Review of recent research on L2 digital multimodal composing. *Computer-Assisted Language Learning and Teaching* 11 (3), 1–16. https://doi.org/10.4018/IJCALLT.2021070101

Li, M. and Zhang, M. (eds) (2023) *L2 Collaborative Writing in Diverse Learning Contexts*. John Benjamins.

Li, S., Hiver, P. and Papi, M. (eds) (2022a) *The Routledge Handbook of Second Language Acquisition and Individual Differences*. Routledge.

Li, S., Hiver, P. and Papi, M. (2022b) Individual differences in second language acquisition: Theory, research, and practice. In S. Li, P. Hiver and M. Papi (eds) *The Routledge Handbook of Second Language Acquisition and Individual Differences* (pp. 3–33). Routledge.

Li, Y. and Deng, L. (2019) I am what I have written: A case study of identity construction in and through personal statement writing. *Journal of English for Academic Purposes* 37, 70–87. https://doi.org/10.1016/j.jeap.2018.11.005

Li, Y., Garza, V., Keicher, A. and Popov, V. (2019) Predicting high school teacher use of technology: Pedagogical beliefs, technological beliefs and attitudes, and teacher training. *Technology, Knowledge and Learning* 24, 501–518. https://doi.org/10.1007/s10758-018-9355-2

Liang, M. (2019) Beyond elocution: Multimodal narrative discourse analysis of L2 storytelling. *ReCALL* 31 (1), 56–74. https://doi.org/10.1017/S0958344018000095

Liaw, M.J.-J. and Accurso, K. (2021) Design and opportunity in critical multilingual/multimodal composing pedagogy. In D.-S. Shin, T. Cimasko and Y. Yi (eds) *Multimodal Composing in K-16 ESL and EFL Education* (pp. 89–108). Springer.

Lim, J. and Polio, C. (2020) Multimodal assignments in higher education: Implications for multimodal writing tasks for L2 writers. *Journal of Second Language Writing* 47, 100713. https://doi.org/10.1016/j.jslw.2020.100713

Lim, J. and Kessler, M. (2022) Directions for future research on SLA, L2 writing, and multimodality. In R.M. Manchón and C. Polio (eds) *The Routledge Handbook of Second Language Acquisition and Writing* (pp. 325–338). Routledge.

Lim, J. and Kessler, M. (2023) Multimodal composing and second language acquisition. *Language Teaching*, 1–20. https://doi.org/10.1017/S0261444823000125

Loewen, S., Buttiler, M., Kessler, M. and Trego, D. (2022) Conversation and transcription activities with synchronous video computer-mediated communication: A classroom investigation. *System* 106, 102760. https://doi.org/10.1016/j.system.2022.102760

Long, M.H. (1981) Input, interaction, and second-language acquisition. *Annals of the New York Academy of Sciences* 379 (1), 259–278. https://doi.org/10.1111/j.1749-6632.1981.tb42014.x

Long, M.H. (1996) The role of the linguistic environment in second language acquisition. In W. Ritchie and T.K. Bhatia (eds) *Handbook of Language Acquisition: Second Language Acquisition* (pp. 413–468). Academic Press.

Lowe, R. and Ploetzner, R. (2017) *Learning from Dynamic Visualization: Innovations in Research and Application*. Springer.

MacIntyre, P.D. and Wang, L. (2022) Anxiety. In S. Li, P. Hiver and M. Papi (eds) *The Routledge Handbook of Second Language Acquisition and Individual Differences* (pp. 175–189). Routledge.

Maloney, J. and Kessler, M. (2019) Ethnography: Connecting the local and the global. In P.I. De Costa, D. Crowther and J. Maloney (eds) *Investigating World Englishes: Research Methodology and Practical Applications* (pp. 44–65). Routledge.

Manchón, R.M. (2017) The potential impact of multimodal composition on language learning. *Journal of Second Language Writing* 38, 94–95. https://doi.org/10.1016/j.jslw.2017.10.008

Mao, S.S. and Crosthwaite, P. (2019) Investigating written corrective feedback: (Mis)alignment of teachers' beliefs and practice. *Journal of Second Language Writing* 45, 46–60. https://doi.org/10.1016/j.jslw.2019.05.004

Martel, J. (2019) Three foreign language student teachers' experiences with content-based instruction: Exploring the identity/innovation interface. *Innovation in Language Learning and Teaching* 12 (4), 303–315. https://doi.org/10.1080/17501229.2016.1211134

Matsuda, P.K. (2003) Process and post-process: A discursive history. *Journal of Second Language Writing* 12 (1), 65–83. https://doi.org/10.1016/S1060-3743(02)00127-3

McCulloch, S. (2013) Investigating the reading-to-write processes and source use of L2 postgraduate students in real-life academic tasks: An exploratory study. *Journal of English for Academic Purposes* 12 (2), 136–147. https://doi.org/10.1016/j.jeap.2012.11.009

Mehdiyev, E., Usta, H.G. and Ugurlu, C. (2017) Validity and reliability study: Motivation scale in English. *International Journal of Social Science* 54 (1), 21–37.

Michel, M., Stiefenhöfer, L., Verspoor, M. and Manchón, R.M. (2022) L2 writing processes of language learners in individual and collaborative writing conditions. In R.M. Manchón and C. Polio (eds) *The Routledge Handbook of Second Language Acquisition and Writing* (pp. 67–80). Routledge.

Miller, C.R. (1984) Genre as social action. *Quarterly Journal of Speech* 70 (2), 151–167.

Mitchell, A.E., Jarvis, S., O'Malley, M. and Konstantinova, I. (2015) Working memory measures and L2 proficiency. In Z. (E.) Wen, M.B. Mota and A. McNeill (eds) *Working Memory in Second Language Acquisition and Processing* (pp. 270–284). Multilingual Matters.

Mitsikopoulou, B. (2022) Integrating multimodal and digital literacies in foreign language policy design: Two examples from the Greek context. In S. Diamantopoulou and S. Ørevik (eds) *Multimodality in English Language Learning* (pp. 51–66). Routledge.

Molle, D. and Prior, P. (2008) Multimodal genre systems in EAP writing pedagogy: Reflecting on a needs analysis. *TESOL Quarterly* 42 (4), 541–566. https://doi.org/10.1002/j.1545-7249.2008.tb00148.x

Mok, W.E. (1994) Reflecting on reflections: A case study of experienced and inexperienced ESL teachers. *System* 22 (1), 93–111. https://doi.org/10.1016/0346-251X(94)90043-4

Murphy, J. (2003) Task-based learning: The interaction between tasks and learners. *ELT Journal* 57, 352–360. https://doi.org/10.1093/elt/57.4.352

Negretti, R. (2012) Metacognition in student academic writing: A longitudinal study of metacognitive awareness and its relation to task perception and evaluation of performance. *Written Communication* 29 (2), 142–179. https://doi.org/10.1177/0741088312438529

Negretti, R. (2017) Calibrating genre: Metacognitive judgments and rhetorical effectiveness in academic writing by L2 graduate students. *Applied Linguistics* 38 (4), 512–539. https://doi.org/10.1093/applin/amv051

Negretti, R. and Kuteeva, M. (2011) Fostering metacognitive genre awareness in L2 academic reading and writing: A case study of pre-service English teachers. *Journal of Second Language Writing* 20, 95–110. https://doi.org/10.1016/j.jslw.2011.02.002

Negretti, R. and McGrath, L. (2018) Scaffolding genre knowledge and metacognition: Insights from an L2 doctoral research writing course. *Journal of Second Language Writing* 40, 12–31. https://doi.org/10.1016/j.jslw.2017.12.002

Nelson, M. (2006) Mode, meaning, and synaesthesia in multimedia L2 writing. *Language Learning & Technology* 10 (2), 56–76.

Neumann, H., Leu, S. and McDonough, K. (2019) L2 writers' use of outside sources and the related challenges. *Journal of English for Academic Purposes* 38, 106–120. https://doi.org/10.1016/j.jeap.2019.02.002

New London Group (1996) A pedagogy of multiliteracies: Designing social futures. *Harvard Educational Review* 66, 60–92.

Nishioka, H. (2016) Analysing language development in a collaborative digital storytelling project: Sociocultural perspectives. *System* 62, 39–52. https://doi.org/10.1016/j.system.2016.07.001

Normann, A. (2022) Multimodal text making through digital storytelling: EAL student teachers' reflections. In S. Diamantopoulou and S. Ørevik (eds) *Multimodality in English Language Learning* (pp. 190–203). Routledge.

Norton, B. (2013) *Identity and Language Learning: Extending the Conversation*. Multilingual Matters.

O'Byrne, B. and Murrell, S. (2014) Evaluating multimodal literacies in student blogs. *British Journal of Educational Technology* 45 (5), 926–940. https://doi.org/10.1111/bjet.12093

Ong, J. (2014) How do planning time and task conditions affect metacognitive processes of L2 writers? *Journal of Second Language Writing* 23, 17–30. https://doi.org/10.1016/j.jslw.2013.10.002

Ørevik, S. (2022) Developing an assessment framework for multimodal text production in the EAL classroom: The case of persuasive posters. In S. Diamantopoulou and S. Ørevik (eds) *Multimodality in English Language Learning* (pp. 257–271). Routledge.

Ortega, L. (2009) *Understanding Second Language Acquisition*. Hodder Education.

Ortega, L. and Iberri-Shea, G. (2005) Longitudinal research in second language acquisition: Recent trends and future directions. *Annual Review of Applied Linguistics* 25, 26–45. https://doi.org/10.1017/S0267190505000024

Oskoz, A. and Elola, I. (2016) Digital stories: Bringing multimodal texts to the Spanish writing classroom. *ReCALL* 28 (3), 326–342. https://doi.org/10.1017/S0958344016000094

Palak, D. and Walls, R.T. (2014) Teachers' beliefs and technology practices. *Journal of Research on Technology in Education* 41 (4), 417–441. https://doi.org/10.1080/15391523.2009.10782537

Paltridge, B. and Phakiti, A. (2015) *Research Methods in Applied Linguistics: A Practical Resource*. Bloomsbury.

Papi, M. and Hiver, P. (2022) Motivation. In S. Li, P. Hiver and M. Papi (eds) *The Routledge Handbook of Second Language Acquisition and Individual Differences* (pp. 113–127). Routledge.

Papi, M., Vasylets, O. and Ahmadian, M.J. (2022) Individual difference factors for second language writing. In S. Li, P. Hiver and M. Papi (eds) *The Routledge Handbook of Second Language Acquisition and Individual Differences* (pp. 381–395). Routledge.

Park, H. (2021) 'Dear future me': Connecting college L2 writers' literacy paths to an envisioned future self through a multimodal project. In D.-S. Shin, T. Cimasko and Y. Yi (eds) *Multimodal Composing in K-16 ESL and EFL Education* (pp. 73–86). Springer.

Park, J. and De Costa, P.I. (2015) Reframing graduate student writing strategies from an Activity Theory perspective. *Language and Sociocultural Theory* 2 (1), 25–50. https://doi.org/10.1558/lst.v2i1.24977

Peng, J. (2022) Willingness to communicate. In S. Li, P. Hiver and M. Papi (eds) *The Routledge Handbook of Second Language Acquisition and Individual Differences* (pp. 159–172). Routledge.

Perez, M.M. (2020) Multimodal input in SLA research. *Studies in Second Language Acquisition* 42 (3), 653–663. https://doi.org/10.1017/S0272263120000145

Pintrich, P.R. (2002) The role of metacognitive knowledge in learning, teaching, and assessing. *Theory into Practice* 41 (4), 219–225. https://doi.org/10.1207/s15430421tip4104_3

Pintrich, P.R. (2004) A conceptual framework for assessing motivation and self-regulated learning in college students. *Educational Psychology Review* 16 (4), 385–407. https://doi.org/10.1007/s10648-004-0006-x

Plakans, L. and Gebril, A. (2015) *Assessment Myths: Applying Second Language Research to Classroom Teaching*. The University of Michigan Press.

Plonsky, L. and Ghanbar, H. (2018) Multiple regression in L2 research: A methodological synthesis and guide to interpreting $R^2$ values. *The Modern Language Journal* 102 (4), 713–731. https://doi.org/10.1111/modl.12509

Polio, C. (2017) Thinking allowed: Second language writing development: A research agenda. *Language Teaching* 50 (2), 261–275. https://doi.org/10.1017/S0261444817000015

Polio, C. and Kessler, M. (2019) Teaching L2 writing: Connecting SLA theory, research, and pedagogy. In N. Polat, P. MacIntyre and T. Gregersen (eds) *Research-Driven Pedagogy: Implications of L2A Theory and Research for the Teaching of Language Skills* (pp. 76–96). Routledge.

Polio, C. and Yoon, H.-J. (2024) Complexity, accuracy, and fluency (CALF) measures. In M. Kessler and C. Polio (eds) *Conducting Genre-Based Research in Applied Linguistics: A Methodological Guide* (pp. 149–171). Routledge.

Porte, G. (ed.) (2012) *Replication Research in Applied Linguistics*. Cambridge University Press.

Porte, G. and McManus, K. (2018) *Doing Replication Research in Applied Linguistics*. Routledge.

Priego, S. and Liaw, M. (2017) Understanding different levels of group functionality: Activity systems analysis of an intercultural telecollaborative multilingual digital storytelling project. *Computer Assisted Language Learning* 30 (5), 368–389. https://doi.org/10.1080/09588221.2017.1306567

Pyo, J. (2016) Bridging in-school and out-of-school literacies: An adolescent EL's composition of a multimodal project. *Journal of Adolescent and Adult Literacy* 59 (4), 421–430. https://doi.org/10.1002/jaal.467

Qu, W. (2017) For L2 writers, it is always the problem of the language. *Journal of Second Language Writing* 38, 92–93. https://doi.org/10.1016/j.jslw.2017.10.007

Rose, D. and Martin, J. (2012) *Learning to Write, Reading to Learn: Genre, Knowledge and Pedagogy of the Sydney School*. Equinox.

Ryu, J. and Boggs, G. (2016) Teachers' perceptions about teaching multimodal composition: The case study of Korean English teachers at secondary schools. *English Language Teaching* 9 (6), 52–60.

Sato, M. (2022) Metacognition. In S. Li, P. Hiver and M. Papi (eds) *The Routledge Handbook of Second Language Acquisition and Individual Differences* (pp. 95–110). Routledge.

Sato, M. and Loewen, S. (2019) Do teachers care about research? The research-pedagogy dialogue. *ELT Journal* 73 (1), 1–10. https://doi.org/10.1093/elt/ccy048

Sato, M., Loewen, S. and Pastushenkov, D. (2022) 'Who is my research for?': Researcher perceptions of the research-practice relationship. *Applied Linguistics* 43 (4), 625–652. https://doi.org/10.1093/applin/amab079

Schmidt, R. (1990) The role of consciousness in second language learning. *Applied Linguistics* 11 (2), 129–158. https://doi.org/10.1093/applin/11.2.129

Schraw, G. (1998) Promoting general metacognitive awareness. *Instructional Science* 26, 113–125. https://doi.org/10.1023/A:1003044231033

Schraw, G. and Dennison, R.S. (1994) Assessing metacognitive awareness. *Contemporary Educational Psychology* 19, 460–475. https://doi.org/10.1006/ceps.1994.1033

Schrieber, B. (2015) 'I am what I am': Multilingual identity and digital translanguaging. *Language Learning & Technology* 19 (3), 69–87.

Serafini, F. and Gee, E. (eds) (2017) *Remixing Multiliteracies: Theory and Practice from New London to New Times.* Teachers College Press.

Shehadeh, A. (2011) Effects and students' perceptions of collaborative writing in L2. *Journal of Second Language Writing* 20 (4), 286–305. https://doi.org/10.1016/j.jslw.2011.05.010

Shin, D. and Cimasko, T. (2008) Multimodal composition in a college ESL class: New tools, traditional norms. *Computers and Composition* 25 (4), 376–395. https://doi.org/10.1016/j.compcom.2008.07.001

Shin, D., Cimasko, T. and Yi, Y. (2020) Development of metalanguage for multimodal composing: A case study of an L2 writer's design of multimedia texts. *Journal of Second Language Writing* 47, 100714. https://doi.org/10.1016/j.jslw.2020.100714

Sindoni, M.G., Moschini, I., Adami, E. and Karatza, S. (2022) The common framework for reference for intercultural digital literacies (CFRIDiL): Learning as meaning-making and assessment as recognition in English as an additional language contexts. In S. Diamantopoulou and S. Ørevik (eds) *Multimodality in English Language Learning* (pp. 221–237). Routledge.

Singleton, D. and Pfenninger, S.E. (2022) Age. In S. Li, P. Hiver and M. Papi (eds) *The Routledge Handbook of Second Language Acquisition and Individual Differences* (pp. 251–265). Routledge.

Smith, B.E., Pacheco, M.B. and de Almeida, C.R. (2017) Multimodal codemeshing: Bilingual adolescents' processes composing across modes and languages. *Journal of Second Language Writing* 36, 6–22. https://doi.org/10.1016/j.jslw.2017.04.001

Stapleton, P. and Radia, P. (2010) Tech-era L2 writing: Towards a new kind of process. *ELT Journal* 64 (2), 175–183. https://doi.org/10.1093/elt/ccp038

Storch, N. (2019) Research timeline: Collaborative writing. *Language Teaching* 52 (1), 40–59. https://doi.org/10.1017/S0261444818000320

Storch, N. (2022) Theoretical perspectives on L2 writing and language learning in collaborative writing and the collaborative processing of written corrective feedback. In R.M. Manchón and C. Polio (eds) *The Routledge Handbook of Second Language Acquisition and Writing* (pp. 22–34). Routledge.

Storch, N. and Aldosari, A. (2013) Pairing learners in pair work activity. *Language Teaching Research* 17 (1), 31–48. https://doi.org/10.1177/1362168812457530

Supasiraprapa, S. and De Costa, P.I. (2017) Metadiscourse and identity construction in teaching philosophy statements: A critical case study of two MATESOL students. *TESOL Quarterly* 51 (4), 868–896. https://doi.org/10.1002/tesq.360

Sun, Y., Yang, K. and Silva, T. (2021) Multimodality in L2 writing: Intellectual roots and contemporary developments. In D.-S. Shin, T. Cimasko and Y. Yi (eds) *Multimodal Composing in K-16 ESL and EFL Education* (pp. 3–16). Springer.

Swain, M. (1985) Communicative competence: Some roles of comprehensible input and comprehensible output in its development. In S. Gass and C. Madden (eds) *Input in Second Language Acquisition* (pp. 235–253). Newbury House.

Swain, M. (1993) The output hypothesis: Just speaking and writing aren't enough. *Canadian Modern Language Review* 50 (1), 158–164. https://doi.org/10.3138/cmlr.50.1.158

Swain, M. (1995) Three functions of output in second language learning. In G. Cook and B. Seidlhofer (eds) *Principle and Practice in Applied Linguistics* (pp. 125–144). Oxford University Press.

Swain, M. and Lapkin, S. (1998) Interaction and second language learning: Two adolescent French immersion students working together. *The Modern Language Journal* 82 (3), 320–337. https://doi.org/10.1111/j.1540-4781.1998.tb01209.x

Swales, J.M. (1990) *Genre Analysis: English in Academic and Research Settings*. Cambridge University Press.

Swales, J.M. (2004) *Research Genres: Exploration and Applications*. Cambridge University Press.

Sydorenko, T., Hsieh, C.-H., Ahn, S. and Arnold, N. (2017) Foreign language learners' beliefs about CALL: The case of a U.S. Midwestern University. *CALICO Journal* 34, 196–218. https://www.jstor.org/stable/90014688

Tahmouresi, S. and Papi, M. (2021) Future selves, enjoyment and anxiety as predictors of L2 writing achievement. *Journal of Second Language Writing* 53, 100837. https://doi.org/10.1016/j.jslw.2021.100837

Tan, X. and Matsuda, P.K. (2020) Teacher beliefs and pedagogical practices of integrating multimodality into first-year composition. *Computers and Composition* 58, 102614. https://doi.org/10.1016/j.compcom.2020.102614

Tardy, C. (2005) Expressions of disciplinarity and individuality in a multimodal genre. *Computers and Composition* 22 (3), 319–336. https://doi.org/10.1016/j.compcom.2005.05.004

Thang, S.M., Sim, L.Y., Mahmud, N., Lin, L.K., Zabidi, N.A. and Ismail, K. (2014) Enhancing 21st century learning skills via digital storytelling: Voices of Malaysian teachers and undergraduates. *Procedia: Social and Behavioral Sciences* 118, 489–494. https://doi.org/10.1016/j.sbspro.2014.02.067

Tobin, L. (1994) Introduction: How the writing process was born – And other conversion narratives. In L. Tobin and T. Newkirk (eds) *Taking Stock: The Writing Process Movement in the '90s* (pp. 1–14). Boynton/Cook Heinemann.

Tomlinson, B. (2022) Materials development for language learning: Ways of connecting practice and theory in coursebook development and use. In E. Hinkel (ed.) *Handbook of Practical Second Language Teaching and Learning* (pp. 133–147). Routledge.

Torrance, E.P. (1998) *Torrance Tests of Creative Thinking: Norms-Technical Manual: Figural (Streamlined) Forms A & B*. Scholastic Testing Service.

Towndrow, P.A., Nelson, M.E. and Yusuf, W.F.B.M. (2013) Squaring literacy assessment with multimodal design: An analytic case for semiotic awareness. *Journal of Literacy Research* 45 (4), 327–355. https://doi.org/10.1177/1086296X13504155

Tseng, M.L. (2021) Exploring pre-service EFL teachers' learning of reflective writing from a multimodal composing perspective: From inter-semiotic complementarity to the learning transfer of genre knowledge. In D.-S. Shin, T. Cimasko and Y. Yi (eds) *Multimodal Composing in K-16 ESL and EFL Education* (pp. 125–144). Springer.

Unsworth, L. and Mills, K.A. (2020) English language teaching of attitude and emotion in digital multimodal composition. *Journal of Second Language Writing* 47, 1–17. https://doi.org/10.1016/j.jslw.2020.100712

Van Leeuwen, T. (2005) *Introducing Social Semiotics*. Routledge.

Vandommele, G., Van den Branden, K., Van Gorp, K. and De Maeyer, S. (2017) In-school and out-of-school multimodal writing as an L2 writing resource for beginner learners of Dutch. *Journal of Second Language Writing* 36, 23–36. https://doi.org/10.1016/j.jslw.2017.05.010

VanPatten, B. and Williams, J. (2015) Introduction: The nature of theories. In B. VanPatten and J. Williams (eds) *Theories in Second Language Acquisition: An Introduction* (pp. 1–16). Routledge.

VanPatten, B., Keating, G.D. and Wulff, S. (eds) (2020) *Theories in Second Language Acquisition* (3rd edn). Routledge.

Vygotsky, L.S. (1978) *Mind in Society: The Development of Higher Psychological Processes*. Harvard University Press.

Waller, L. and Papi, M. (2017) Motivation and feedback: How implicit theories of intelligence predict L2 writers' motivation and feedback orientation. *Journal of Second Language Writing* 35, 54–65. https://doi.org/10.1016/j.jslw.2017.01.004

Wei, X. (2020) Assessing the metacognitive awareness relevant to L1-to-L2 rhetorical transfer in L2 writing: The cases of Chinese EFL writers across proficiency levels. *Assessing Writing* 44, 100452. https://doi.org/10.1016/j.asw.2020.100452

Wenden, A.L. (1991) Metacognitive strategies in L2 writing: A case for task knowledge. In J.E. Alatis (ed.) *Georgetown University Roundtable on Languages and Linguistics 1991: Linguistics and Language Pedagogy: The State of the Art* (pp. 302–322). Georgetown University Press.

Wertsch, J.V. (1985) *Vygotsky and the Social Formation of Mind*. Harvard University Press.

Williams, J. (2012) The potential role(s) of writing in second language development. *Journal of Second Language Writing* 21 (4), 321–331. https://doi.org/10.1016/j.jslw.2012.09.007

Winke, P. and Goertler, S. (2008) Did we forget someone? Students' computer access and literacy for CALL. *CALICO Journal* 25 (3), 482–509. https://www.jstor.org/stable/calicojournal.25.3.482

Winke, P. and Brunfaut, T. (2021) *The Routledge Handbook of Second Language Acquisition and Language Testing*. Routledge.

Winke, P., Lee, S., Ahn, J.I., Choi, I., Cui, Y. and Yoon., H.-J. (2018) The cognitive validity of child English language tests: What young language learners and their native-speaking peers can reveal. *TESOL Quarterly* 52 (2), 274–303. https://doi.org/10.1002/tesq.396

Wu, J.J. and Cherng, B.L. (1992) Motivated strategies for learning questionnaire (MSLQ): A revised version for use with Chinese elementary and junior high school students. *Psychological Testing* 39, 59–78.

Xi, J. and Lantolf, J.P. (2021) Scaffolding and the zone of proximal development: A problematic relationship. *Journal of the Theory of Social Behavior* 51 (1), 25–48. https://doi.org/10.1111/jtsb.12260

Xu, Y. (2021) Investigating the effects of digital multimodal composing on Chinese EFL learners' writing performance: A quasi-experimental study. *Computer Assisted Language Learning*, 1–21. https://doi.org/10.1080/09588221.2021.1945635

Yang, Y.-F. (2012) Multimodal composing in digital storytelling. *Computers and Composition* 29 (3), 221–238. https://doi.org/10.1016/j.compcom.2012.07.001

Yang, Y.-T.C. and Wu, W.-C.I. (2012) Digital storytelling for enhancing student academic achievement, critical thinking, and learning motivation: A year-long experimental study. *Computers & Education* 59 (2), 339–352. https://doi.org/10.1016/j.compedu.2011.12.012

Yang, Y.-T.C., Chen, Y.-C. and Hung, H.-T. (2020) Digital storytelling as an interdisciplinary project to improve students' English speaking and creative thinking. *Computer Assisted Language Learning* 35 (4), 840–862. https://doi.org/10.1080/09588221.2020.1750431

Yeh, E. and Mitric, S. (2019) Voices to be heard: Using social media for digital storytelling to foster language learners' engagement. *TESL-EJ* 24 (2), 1–15.

Yeh, H.-C. (2015) Facilitating metacognitive processes of academic genre-based writing using an online system. *Computer Assisted Language Learning* 28 (6), 478–498. https://doi.org/10.1080/09588221.2014.881384

Yeh, H.-C. (2018) Exploring the perceived benefits of the process of multimodal video making in developing multiliteracies. *Language Learning & Technology* 22 (2), 28–37. https://doi.org/10125/44642

Yeh, H.-C. and Tseng, S.-S. (2020) Enhancing multimodal literacy using augmented reality. *Language Learning & Technology* 24 (1), 27–37. https://doi.org/10125/44706

Yeh, Y.C. (2003) *Critical Thinking Test-Level I (CTT-I)*. Psychological Publishing.

Yi, Y. and Angay-Crowder, T. (2016) Multimodal pedagogies for teacher education in TESOL. *TESOL Quarterly* 50 (4), 988–998. https://doi.org/10.1002/tesq.326

Yi, Y., King, N. and Safriani, A. (2017) Reconceptualizing assessment for digital multimodal literacy. *TESOL Journal* 8 (4), 878–885. https://doi.org/10.1002/tesj.354

Yu, S., Jiang, L. and Zhou, N. (2020) The impact of L2 writing instructional approaches on student writing motivation and engagement. *Language Teaching Research*. https://doi.org/10.1177/1362168820957024

Yuan, R. (2019) A critical review on nonnative English teacher identity research: From 2008 to 2017. *Journal of Multilingual and Multicultural Development* 40 (6), 518–537. https://doi.org/10.1080/01434632.2018.1533018

Zhang, Z. (2020) Engaging with automated writing evaluation (AWE) feedback on L2 writing: Student perceptions and revisions. *Assessing Writing* 43, 100439. https://doi.org/10.1016/j.asw.2019.100439

Zhang, Y. and O'Halloran, K. (2019) Empowering the point: Pains and gains of a writer's traversals between print-based writing and multimodal composing. *Linguistics and Education* 51, 1–11. https://doi.org/10.1016/j.linged.2019.04.003

Zhang, M., Akoto, M. and Li, M. (2023) Digital multimodal composing in post-secondary L2 settings: A review of the empirical landscape. *Computer Assisted Language Learning* 36 (4), 694–721. https://doi.org/10.1080/09588221.2021.1942068

# Index

3D maps 96, 101-102, 106, 115

Accuracy 29, 42, 46, 50, 52-56, 72-73
Activity Theory 20-21, 35, 122-123
Anxiety 67, 77, 84-85, 88-89, 129
Argumentative essay 35, 37-38, 41-42, 51-52, 54, 68, 92, 96-98, 106

Blog 6, 42, 44, 69, 88-90, 96-98, 106-107, 120, 127

Chinese (China) 4-5, 35, 54, 70, 80-83, 114, 124
Classroom observation 33, 39-40, 63, 66, 79, 80-82, 91
Claymation 47, 96, 98-99
Collaborative writing 21, 26, 30, 39, 41, 44, 57, 82
Collective scaffolding 14, 19, 24-26, 48, 92
Comics 3, 97-98, 106
Complexity 42, 46, 50, 52, 55-56, 64, 72-73, 126
Control group 50, 54-55, 57, 83-84

Digital postcard 97-98, 106
Digital poster 6, 24, 35, 49, 51, 58-59, 75, 90, 96, 99, 102-103, 106, 112-114, 130

English for Academic Purposes (EAP) 24, 69-70, 103
Ethnography (ethnographic) 40-41, 62, 81, 84, 128

Fluency 42, 46, 53, 55-56, 73
French (France) 18, 25-26, 82, 124

Gender 40, 84, 91
Genre-based 14, 113-116
Gesture 3, 17, 23, 38, 47, 112
Graded reader 47, 53, 59

Identity 71, 78-82, 88-90, 125, 128-129
Infographics 68-69, 96, 103-104, 106
Interactionist Approaches 17-19, 52, 122-123

Japanese (Japan) 4, 32, 47

Korean (South Korea) 32, 51, 53, 63, 68, 72, 79

Language-related episodes (LREs) 32-33, 41-43
Listening skills 18, 51, 58-59, 84, 125-128
Longitudinal 40, 57, 80, 87, 125-126

Metacognition 21-23, 46, 56-57, 86-88, 104-105, 122-123, 128-129
Mind maps 32, 118
Motivation 46, 56, 63, 65, 77, 82-85, 88-90, 128-129
Multiliteracies 16-17, 23, 47, 53, 63, 68, 79, 81, 111-112, 116, 122
Multimodal visualization 87-88, 91-92, 96, 98-99, 104-106

Noticing Hypothesis (noticing) 17-18, 30, 50-51, 75

Output Hypothesis (output) 17-18, 52-53, 109, 126

Quasi-experimental 49, 52, 57, 89, 126, 128
Questionnaire 67, 83, 85-86, 70

Reading skills 18, 64, 84, 125-128
Remix 14, 24, 35-37, 44
Replication (replicate) 58, 124
Research proposal 35, 92, 96-98, 106, 127
Rubric 54, 65, 110-118, 120

Semi-structured interview 62-63, 69-70, 80, 112
Slideshow (slideshow presentation) 5, 49, 79, 96-99, 107, 111-112
Social Semiotics 5, 15-17, 31, 37, 122, 124
Sociocultural Theory 19-20, 25, 32, 83, 122-124
Soundtrack 3, 36, 80, 101, 119

Spanish 66-67
Spatial 3, 17, 23, 47, 109, 112
Speaking skills 52-53, 59, 125-127
Storyboard 31, 46-47, 52-53, 60, 68, 80, 96-99, 105, 107, 117-118, 120
Survey 48, 51-52, 63-64, 68, 112, 125
Systemic Functional Linguistics (SFL) 14-15, 39, 122-123

T-test 40, 51-52, 56, 85
Taiwanese (Taiwan) 31, 34, 48, 52, 67, 83, 86, 111
Task-Based Language Teaching (TBLT) 10, 13, 62
Transformation activity (transform) 24, 35-39, 41-42, 51, 58-59, 103

Willingness to communicate 77, 80-81, 88-89, 129

For Product Safety Concerns and Information please contact our EU Authorised Representative:

Easy Access System Europe

Mustamäe tee 50

10621 Tallinn

Estonia

gpsr.requests@easproject.com

www.ingramcontent.com/pod-product-compliance
Ingram Content Group UK Ltd.
Pitfield, Milton Keynes, MK11 3LW, UK
UKHW021834140426
5217IPUK00021B/1449